D1189402

Utah
CURIOSITIES

QUIRKY CHARACTERS, ROADSIDE ODDITIES & OTHER OFFBEAT STUFF

BRANDON GRIGGS

INSIDERS' GUIDE®

GUILFORD, CONNECTICUT
AN IMPRINT OF THE GLOBE PEQUOT PRESS

To buy books in quantity for corporate use
or incentives, call **(800) 962–0973**
or e-mail **premiums@GlobePequot.com.**

INSIDERS' GUIDE®

Copyright © 2008 by Morris Book Publishing, LLC

All rights reserved. No part of this book may be reproduced or transmitted in any form
by any means, electronic or mechanical, including photocopying and recording, or by
any information storage and retrieval system, except as may be expressly permitted by
the 1976 Copyright Act or by the publisher. Requests for permission should be made in
writing to The Globe Pequot Press, P.O. Box 480, Guilford, Connecticut 06437.

Insiders' Guide is a registered trademark of Morris Book Publishing, LLC.

Text design by Nancy Freeborn
Layout by Debbie Nicolais
Maps created by Rusty Nelson © Morris Book Publishing, LLC

Photo credits: pp. 6, 69, 153, 155, 172, 188, 201, 251 Courtesy of the Utah Historical
Society; p. 10 Francisco Kjolseth/*The Salt Lake Tribune;* p. 12 Steve Griffin/*The Salt Lake
Tribune;* p. 17 Rick Egan/*The Salt Lake Tribune;* pp. 24, 129 Al Hartmann/*The Salt Lake
Tribune;* p. 27 Courtesy of Paramount Pictures; p. 56 Doug Carter; pp. 78, 132, 217 Leah
Hogsten/*The Salt Lake Tribune;* pp. 113, 114 Courtesy of The Maize; p. 116 Courtesy of
Homestead Resort; pp. 123, 124 Courtesy of Olympic Parks of Utah; p. 127 Courtesy of
the Monte Bean Life Sciences Museum; p. 192 Arva Dale Ashman; p. 221 Chris
Detrick/*The Salt Lake Tribune;* p. 248 The National Park Service; p. 266 Courtesy of the
Paunsaugunt Wildlife Museum; p. 269 Karl Hugh/Utah Shakespearean Festival; p. 279
Molly Wald/Best Friends Animal Society, and p. 306 Kristy Griggs. All other photos are
by the author.

Library of Congress Cataloging-in-Publication Data is available.
ISBN: 978-0-7627-4386-5

Manufactured in the United States of America
First Edition/Second Printing

For my incredible wife Kristy, who put up with her husband for six months while he hit the road, hogged our computer, and fussed over this book. I couldn't have done it without your unwavering love, patience, and support.

UTAH

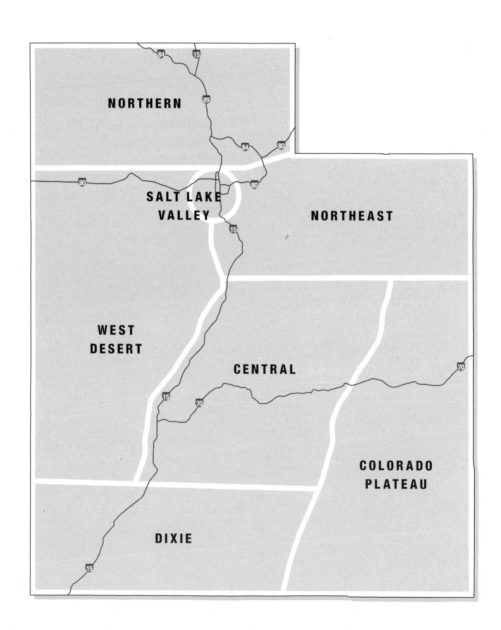

Contents

Acknowledgments

My deepest gratitude to my fellow road warriors Marc Zolton, Rudy Mesicek, and Kristy Griggs, who accompanied me, without complaint, around Utah's back highways to help me gather material for this book. You were great company and I'd hit the road with you again anytime.

Thanks also to Tom Wharton and Pete Giacoma (and his fine staff at the Davis County Library) for all your research tips, suggestions, and enthusiasm for this project. I owe you guys a beer.

Finally, many thanks and much love to my mother, who has long encouraged me to write a book. This one is just the start.

Easter Island? No, this stone face lives in Red Canyon, near Bryce National Park.

Introduction

As people who've never been there will tell you, Utah is a strange state. Tell a coastal sophisticate you live in Utah, and if you're not greeted by a blank stare of disinterest, they'll lift an eyebrow or crinkle their nose and ask, "What's that like?" as if you just admitted being from Mars.

What these people usually mean is something like, "How can you stand living in such a backwards place, full of squares and sister wives, where everyone looks like an Osmond, you can't get a drink, and there's nothing to do but ski, scrapbook, and go to church?"

It's an ignorant question, but in their own misinformed way, they have a point. There are a few states whose image and culture are so distinct from the rest of the nation that they could almost be separate colonies. Texas is one. Utah is another.

I never planned to live in Salt Lake City. In the summer of 1993 I was living contentedly enough in Washington, D.C., and if you had told me I was about to move to Utah, I would have laughed until I cried. It wasn't on my radar as a potentially cool place to live. That changed when I fell hard for a woman who lived in Park City, the ski-resort town. Within a few months I'd quit my job, packed my car, and headed west, where I soon found work writing features for *The Salt Lake Tribune*. A month after that, my new love dumped me. Two months after that she left Park City and returned to Washington. We'd switched places on the map, leaving me alone in a strange new place.

I was fast learning just how strange it was.

Coming from D.C. I noticed several things at once about the people of Utah. First, Utahns, as they like to be called, are remarkably friendly. Store clerks chirp, "Have a nice day!" and actually seem to mean it. Of course, as a big-city Easterner, I viewed this behavior with great suspicion. Second, most Utahns are incredibly polite. You can stand at a crosswalk in Salt Lake City and just *think* about crossing the street, and motorists will brake for you. Freaky.

My job with the newspaper took me all over the state. I wrote about sailors on the briny waters of the Great Salt Lake, movie stars at the Sundance Film Festival in Park City, ice fishermen on the frozen Jordanelle reservoir, Navajo football players in Monument Valley, and an unorthodox women's conservation group in Moab called Great Old Broads for Wilderness. I knew I'd made it as a feature writer in Utah when, after five years, I finally interviewed Donny Osmond.

And I surprised myself by how much I liked it here.

I've now spent more than a dozen years behind the Zion Curtain, so to speak, and I'm not the same person I was before I came. I've learned to enjoy Utah's amazing scenery, its vast open spaces, and the panoramic skies that show you the coming weather. I've grown to appreciate the patience and decency of its people. I've made great friends in Utah, and I met my beautiful wife here. Somewhere along the way, part of me has been transformed from an Easterner into a Westerner.

So when I hear folks making fun of Utah or my fellow Utahns, I get a little defensive. And believe me, outsiders like to make fun of Utah. Sure, we can be a little nutty. And yes, our legislature sometimes does questionable things, like prohibiting state universities from banning guns on campus. This makes us a frequent target for liberal humorists like Bill Maher, who jokes that if there was a reality TV show called "America's Stupidest State," Utah would always finish in the top five.

Most jokes, of course, revolve around Mormons, whose cultural influence is felt throughout the state. (In case you didn't know, the Mormon Church's official name is the Church of Jesus Christ of Latter-day Saints, which nobody uses because it's too long. So most folks say "LDS Church" instead.) Let's be honest: It's hard to talk about Utah without talking about the LDS Church. Mormons make up more than 60 percent of our population and more than 80 percent of our state legislature. And more than a few outsiders believe that they, above all else, are what make our state weird.

Much of this ignorance stems from century-old prejudices towards Mormons as secretive polygamists. A 1922 anti-LDS propaganda film, *Trapped By the Mormons*, depicted a sinister Mormon missionary who seduced women to become plural wives. A persistent early-1900s myth held that Mormons had horns growing from their heads. Some confuse Mormons with the Amish, the religious sect whose members favor plain dress and horse-drawn buggies.

Even today, some visitors still view Mormons as human oddities. Comedians laugh about the sacred undergarments worn by devout Mormons, calling them "magic underpants." Tourists lean over visitor-information counters and whisper, "Point a Mormon out to me." During the 1997 NBA Finals in Salt Lake City, Chicago Bulls coach Phil Jackson described the LDS Church as a "religious cult or sect or whatever it is."

Of course, these presumptions are misguided and unfair. For starters, the LDS Church renounced its practice of plural marriage in 1890, and although Utah still contains a few shadowy polygamous enclaves, the practice is widely frowned upon today. And let's face it, people, those polygamy jokes are pretty tired.

This book is not the place for a discussion of Mormon doctrine or practices, so I'll just say this: In my personal experience, Mormons have the same hopes and dreams and strengths and frailties as any group of people. In other words, they're pretty much like everybody else—only tidier. Have you ever seen a messy building or lawn or *anything* owned by the LDS Church? No, you haven't.

Besides, trying to define Utah through Mormons alone is like trying to define America through those starchy Englishmen who first colonized our shores. The image doesn't fit anymore. Recent Mormon converts are as likely to be African or Polynesian or South American as white. And as immigrants and transplants join our fast-growing state, the Mormon populace has been dropping for years. If current population trends continue, Mormons will be a minority in Utah by 2030, their numbers diluted by waves of Latinos and refugees from Sudan and Eastern Europe.

Now, I'll concede that Utah's infamous liquor laws are a little silly. Visitors to our fair state's bars must buy "memberships" before entering and find another member to "sponsor" them. "I like a place that has a touch of sobriety in the air," said Garrison Keillor once while broadcasting his radio program from Salt Lake City. Well, Mr. Keillor, you'd fit right in here. Contrary to perceptions, however, Utah isn't dry; you can get a drink almost anywhere in the state.

Despite having the youngest population in the nation, Utah will probably never be hip. Cultural trends seem to arrive here a couple of years after hitting New York and San Francisco. But we're no cultural backwater. We've got opera, sushi bars, abstract art, major-league soccer, and movie theaters showing obscure French films. By golly, we've got the Mormon Tabernacle Choir—the oldest and largest Grammy-winning group of all time.

As a matter of fact, our state is full of interesting contradictions. There's the Utah Jazz, for starters. When the team moved here in 1979 from New Orleans, where jazz *is* part of the cultural fabric, nobody thought to change the name. The Beehive State is not considered especially progressive, yet Utah in 1870 became the second state or territory to grant voting rights to women and in 1917 became the second state to elect a Jewish governor. Sure, much of Utah is so politically conservative that residents think gun control means a steady aim. Yet recent two-term Salt Lake City Mayor Rocky Anderson, who supports same-sex marriage and decriminalizing marijuana, is one of the most liberal politicians in the country.

So be careful when you generalize about Utah. We're more complicated than you might think.

Because almost 90 percent of Utahns live in urban areas around Salt

Lake City, vast expanses of the state are almost uninhabited. This makes it easier to appreciate our spectacular and surprisingly varied landscape, which ranges from snow-capped peaks to lush mountain valleys to sweeping desert plains to rugged canyons of red rock to the unique wetlands of the Great Salt Lake.

I'd dare any state, with the possible exception of California, to beat the beauty and diversity of our natural scenery. (So *bring it on*, Oklahoma! Nah, just kidding.) From Landscape Arch near Moab to the Great Stone Face south of Delta, this scenery even supplies some of the curiosities in this book.

As I drove around the state doing research, I realized that when it comes to bizarre roadside attractions —Clem's Gator Ranch, say, or Thimble World—Utah can't hold a candle to tourist magnets like Florida. Maybe it's because most parts of the state don't see enough year-round tourists to support such places. Maybe it's because Mormonism discourages eccentricity. Some of our curiosities aren't immediately obvious.

But don't worry—they're there.

Most offbeat Utah attractions seem to fall into a handful of broad categories: natural wonders, such as 700-foot-high sand dunes; dinosaurs, for which our state is deservedly famous; pioneer history from the mid-to-late 1800s; quirky Mormon sites; colorful characters, past and present, such as Butch Cassidy; and unique businesses such as the Hole N" the Rock, which is . . . well, pretty much what it sounds like.

Some of these people and places are so goofy that they may give you a chuckle. I hope so. Others are more unusual than funny. But they all have a story behind them. I hope you enjoy discovering them half as much as I did.

When you're through with this book you may agree with those folks I described in the first paragraphs of this introduction. You might think: Yeah, Utah *is* a strange state.

But in a good way.

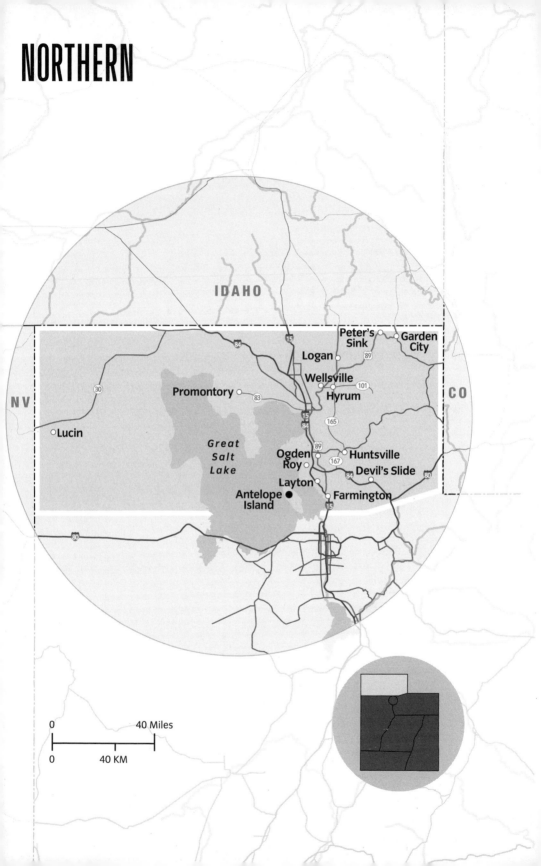

NORTHERN

NORTHERN

If not for Wyoming butting into its northeast corner, Utah would look like a vertical rectangle. Instead, it looks like . . . well . . . an upright La-Z-Boy recliner? A really stubby "L"? The head of some right-angled alien?

Well, that head—basically, from Wyoming's southern border on up—is what this chapter is about. And that's not a bad thing. Northern Utah, the head on the state's blocky shoulders, is chock-full of quirky stuff. There's the Great Salt Lake, for starters. Blessed with birds, brine shrimp and, yes, boatloads of salt, it's like no other place on the planet.

Then there's Ogden, one of the most colorful cities in the American West. Established by a trapper the year before Mormon pioneers reached Salt Lake, it became a major junction city for passenger trains; for decades the streets outside the railroad station buzzed with hotels, restaurants, jazz clubs, and hookers.

The jazz clubs and hookers are mostly gone now, but don't despair—there's still plenty to see around these parts. We've got an escaped pink flamingo, an island full of semi-tamed buffalo, a lake-dwelling monster, and the final resting place of Utah's last grizzly. We've also got a spiral jetty, some sun tunnels, and a 200-foot slide fit for a devil.

Here you can drink in Utah's oldest saloon, gawk at the largest rocket motor ever flown, reenact the joining of the nation's first transcontinental railroad, visit a museum devoted to the Browning family's famous guns, gaze upon the mountain that inspired the Paramount Pictures logo, and ride rickety Old Woodie, a roller coaster that predates Coney Island's Cyclone.

So time's a wastin'! Let's get started.

Shouldn't It Be Called Buffalo Island?

Antelope Island

The largest of the Great Salt Lake's ten islands, Antelope Island is home to bighorn sheep, mule deer, bobcats, coyotes, elk and, yes, some pronghorn antelope. Its most famous residents, however, are a free-roaming herd of bison. How did the buffalo get there, you ask? Well, they didn't swim.

The massive herds of buffalo that roamed the American West were largely gone by 1893, when a man named John E. Dooley bought a small private herd and ordered the animals shipped to the island, most of which he owned at the time. But spooked by some horses, the seventeen buffalo stampeded before they could be loaded onto the cattle boat.

Two ranch hands spent four days rounding them up and herding them onto the small flat boat, which was powered by sails and split down the middle by a deck rail that prevented the shaggy beasts from capsizing the boat by all crowding to one side. Even then, they almost tipped over during the crossing, which was done at night so that the sight of the water wouldn't spook the boat's skittish cargo.

Unmolested on the island, the bison multiplied. By 1925 the original seventeen buffalo had grown into a herd of almost 500. A bunch of finicky eaters, they would ignore the island's range grass in favor of farm potatoes they'd dig up with their hooves.

The state of Utah bought the north tip of the island in 1969 and the rest in 1981, turning it into a state park. The buffalo came with the deal. The herd, now maintained at a steady 600 or so, is culled each November during the Bison Range Ride and Roundup. Men and women on horseback herd the bison into a corral, where vets assess the health of each animal. Spectators are welcome. Several weeks later, the excess buffalo are sold at auction.

Because buffalo are big and ornery animals, herding them is not as easy as it might seem.

"When they want to stop, they stop," one wrangler told the *Salt Lake Tribune* in 2006. "Call it a siesta or whatever, but right around the middle of the day they just lay down. We tried to get some moving during their nap time once, and that was a big mistake."

Visitors can search for the buffalo year-round by taking exit 332 off Interstate 15 near Syracuse and heading west across a causeway to the island. The park's entrance fee is $9 per vehicle. Facilities include a beach picnic area, marina, primitive campground, and a seasonal restaurant that serves—I'm not kidding—buffalo burgers.

In 2093 the herd will celebrate its "bison"-tennial. For more information on the buffalo and the island, call the state park ranger station at (801) 773-2941.

That Devil Sure Knows How To Have Fun

Devil's Slide

Tell kids you're taking them to the Devil's Slide and you're bound to get their attention. They might be disappointed upon arrival at this peculiar rock formation that they can't ride the slide, however. Why does the Devil get all the fun, anyway?

The slide is visible from Interstate 84 southeast of Ogden, where motorists gaze up in puzzlement at the mountain-side above the freeway. There, two natural rock walls run parallel, some 25 feet apart, on a straight line down the hill. The walls are 40 feet high, extend for several hundred feet, and were created when erosion whittled away the surrounding softer rock, leaving the twin strips of stubborn limestone.

Why does only the Devil get a slide?

With a little imagination the slide also looks like a rain gutter, or one of those tracks that guides balls back to you at the bowling alley. Nobody seems to know quite how the slide got named for the Devil. Maybe it's because angels, with their wings, don't need to slide down a mountain for kicks.

A nearby mining village was named Devil's Slide after the rock formation, but its population dwindled and it became a ghost town by the 1990s. To see the Devil's Slide, take I-84 from either I-15 near Ogden or Interstate 80 northeast of Park City. There's a scenic viewpoint near mile marker 111.

Swooning over Lagoon
Farmington

Lagoon, the largest amusement park between the Midwest and San Francisco, is not your typical attraction. For one, it's got some serious history: Lagoon is the oldest operating park in the American West and its original roller coaster, nicknamed "Old Woodie," is the third-oldest in the nation—older even than Coney Island's fabled Cyclone.

The park was named for a nine-acre body of water located on its site when it opened in 1896. It was more of a pond than a lagoon, but as an amusement-park name, "Pond" might not have packed in the crowds. The pond was used to harvest ice in the winter.

The original Lagoon offered such thrill-a-minute attractions as bowling, a dance pavilion, and a "shady bowery." Roller-coaster designer John Miller of Coney Island fame built Old Woodie, also known as "the white coaster," in 1921. Reaching a height of 60 feet and speeds of 45 mph, the nearly half-mile-long wooden coaster still produces its share of squeals today.

Six years later the park added a 1.5-million-gallon swimming pool filled with "water fit to drink." One of the first filtered swimming pools in the West, it became a popular alternative to bathing in the briny Great Salt Lake. Much of the park was rebuilt after a 1953 fire that produced flames so high they could be seen 17 miles south in Salt Lake City.

Besides the usual rides, Ferris wheel, and carnival games, Lagoon at one time or another offered boating, horse racing, a miniature railroad, an opera house, hot-air balloon rides, rodeos, baseball games, boxing matches, a zoo, Wild West shows, blackface minstrel shows, and a roller coaster called Colossus the Fire Dragon.

Lagoon, one of the oldest amusement parks in the country, has a colorful history.

In the 1970s the park added a pioneer village filled with early Mormon artifacts, including extensive collections of antique guns, carriages, and model trains, plus a handful of historic buildings moved there from other locations.

Although Lagoon no longer books concerts, the park over the decades has hosted a remarkable assortment of musical and comedy acts, from Duke Ellington and the Three Stooges to Jimi Hendrix, Janis Joplin, the Doors, and the Beach Boys. The California surfer band returned the favor by referencing Lagoon in their song, "Salt Lake City."

Accessed from exit 325 off I-15, Lagoon is open April through October. For more information, call (801) 451-8000 or visit www.lagoon park.com.

Move Over Nessie, It's The Bear Lake Monster
Garden City

Bear Lake, a 22-mile-long expanse on the Utah-Idaho border, is famous for its crystalline blue sheen, water sports, and seasonal raspberries. Oh yeah, and the serpent-like creature dwelling in its 200-foot depths.

The legend of the Bear Lake Monster dates to an 1868 published report in a Salt Lake City newspaper by Bear Lake store owner Joseph C. Rich, who cited accounts by people who saw a huge brown creature swimming through the water "faster than a horse could run."

Twenty years later, Rich admitted to making up the tale. But the mystique of the mysterious beast wouldn't die. Brigham Young himself peered into the lake in search of a glimpse. Over the next century, occasional sightings kept the legend alive. One local newspaper even printed a tale of the creature devouring an entire Mormon family.

Trouble was, nobody seemed to agree on exactly what the monster looked like: "A body half-seal, half-serpent, and a head somewhat like a sea lion." "About 20 feet in length, with a mouth sufficiently large to swallow a man without any difficulty." "Not less than 90 feet in length." "Part dragon, part bear, and part fish." Brown. Green. Cream-colored.

Rumors and wild theories ran rampant. Some people speculated that an underground waterway connected Bear Lake to Loch Ness, Scotland, allowing the monster to go back and forth.

An extensive sonar sounding of the lake in 2002 found no evidence of a large creature swimming in its waters. But that same summer, a watercraft-rental shop owner named Brian Hirschi reported seeing the monster. Hirschi said he was anchoring a boat alone at dusk when an "enormous slimy green creature with red eyes" shot out of the water nearby, "squealing and roaring like a bull."

Skeptics note the only people who seem to encounter the monster firsthand are local business owners who thrive on the tourism such a fish story provides. That includes Hirschi, who runs the Bear Lake Monster Boat, a 65-foot green pontoon vessel with a dragon's head. The boat offers summertime tours of the lake, departing from Ideal Beach Marina south of town, that include stories about the monster's legend. For information, call Performance Rental at (435) 946-8735.

Also near Garden City:

The Pickleville Playhouse, a goofy lakeshore theater that stages musicals and original comedies each summer. Find out more at (435) 946-2918 or www.picklevilleplayhouse.com.

SOME REALLY SHRIMPY SHRIMP

What lives in the waters of the Great Salt Lake, which are five times saltier than the ocean? Almost nothing except millions of tiny critters called brine shrimp. Before you get visions of a tasty shrimp cocktail—a margarita version, perhaps—you should know these little invertebrates are about the size of a large ant. A key part of the lake's food chain, they munch on algae and serve as a crucial snack for the many migrating birds that visit the lake each year. If you wade into the lake and peer closely into the water, you can spot them swimming around.

Known also as artemia or even "sea monkeys," the brine shrimp are notable for several things: When they die, their little husks wash up in piles on the lake's beaches, attracting swarms of brine flies in summer that can put a quick end to any picnic. They also are harvested each fall for their red eggs, or cysts, which are sold to feed farm-raised fish and prawns throughout the world.

In 1976 a Utah filmmaker shot a sixteen-minute movie, *Attack of the Giant Brine Shrimp,* featuring a mutant lake creature that terrorized the people of downtown Salt Lake City. The shrimp scaled the towers of the city's Mormon Temple until a giant seagull swooped in and gobbled it.

The Spiral Jetty
Great Salt Lake

On the remote northern shore of the Great Salt Lake, some 40 miles from the nearest town, lies one of the world's largest and most bizarre artworks. It's called the Spiral Jetty, and it was created by New Jersey sculptor Robert Smithson in 1970 during a time when experimental artists were treating nature like a blank canvas.

Most jetties extend straight into the water. This one curls counterclockwise into a spiral, as if designed by a drunken engineer. It's 15 feet wide, extends 1,500 feet from shore, and is large enough to be visible from space. The jetty's meanings remain a mystery; three years after it was built, Smithson died in a plane crash.

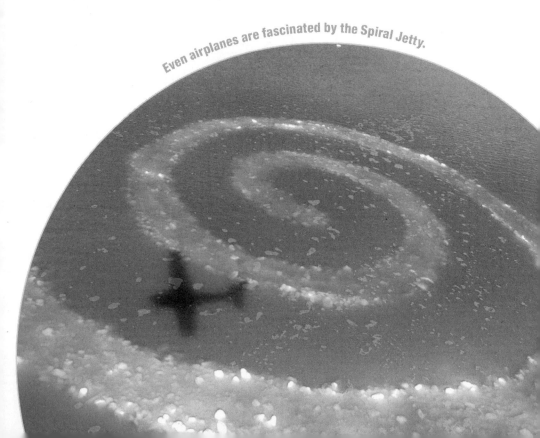

Even airplanes are fascinated by the Spiral Jetty.

To rural Utah construction workers in April 1970, the long-haired Eastern artist with the black leather pants must have seemed like someone from another planet. The contractor thought Smithson's idea was "dumber than a box of rocks." But Smithson had a check for $6,000, and a job is a job. Using rocks from the nearby shoreline, workers built the jetty in a few weeks. Its legend, however, has endured for more than three decades. Art scholars study it, and the *New York Times* calls the jetty "the most famous work of American art that almost nobody has ever seen in the flesh."

Two years after the jetty was built, the rising waters of the lake swallowed it completely. But in recent years the waters have receded, and the rocks once again protrude from the lake's surface. Visitors can walk out onto the jetty or admire it from the hillside above.

A steady trickle of art geeks brave a teeth-rattling dirt road to visit the jetty each month. Because there are few signs pointing the way, many stop for directions at nearby Promontory Point, the spot in 1869 where workers pounded a golden spike to connect the Intercontinental Railroad. The two historic sites make ironic bedfellows: One was crucial to the transportation needs of a young nation, while the other has no practical significance whatsoever.

It is kind of cool, though.

To reach the Spiral Jetty, take Highway 83 west from I-15 north of Brigham City. Shortly after you pass the Golden Spike National Historic Site, turn south on a dirt road marked by a small sign for the jetty. Follow the road to the lakeshore, where you'll find a primitive parking area. On foot, follow the shoreline to the right to the jetty.

THE OTHER PINK FLOYD

If you're bird-watching along the shores of the Great Salt Lake and spot a pink flamingo—a live one, not the kind you see on people's lawns—don't worry that you've spent too much time in the sun. That's just Pink Floyd.

The Chilean flamingo escaped from the Tracy Aviary in Salt Lake City in 1988, flew out to the lake, and has made himself comfortable there ever since. Nicknamed for a certain legendary rock band, he has become something of a cult figure. Bird-watchers spot him there every winter, gobbling brine shrimp and hanging out with a group of seagulls. (Nobody knows exactly where he goes in the summer, although he reportedly has been spotted at reservoirs near the Idaho-Montana border.)

As far as anyone can tell, Floyd is perfectly happy. But some Utahns worry that he gets lonely being the only bird of his species that calls the lake home. In 2003 a group called Friends For Floyd launched a campaign to find Floyd some companions by introducing more tropical flamingos to the Great Salt Lake. The group even offered to pay almost $50,000 to import twenty-five flamingos from South America. So far state officials, citing possible harmful effects to the lake's fragile ecosystem, have refused the offer. So Pink Floyd will have to make do for now with gulls, grebes, plovers, and other native feathered friends.

Look for him the next time you visit the lake. Considering that flamingos can live up to sixty years, Floyd may be around for a while. And we're all grateful for that.

Pink Floyd flew the coop and became a legend.

Beer, Burgers, and a Stuffed St. Bernard

Huntsville

It's hard to say what is the coolest thing about the Shooting Star Saloon. First there's its name, which conjures images of the Old West. There's its history as Utah's oldest continually operating bar. There are the hundreds of dollar bills stapled to its ceiling. And then there's the stuffed head of a giant St. Bernard mounted on the wall.

The dog's head, as you might imagine, comes with a story. Seems its Montana owner was so sad when his 300-pound dog died in the 1950s that he hired a taxidermist to mount its head. But the head was so large the taxidermist had to use a grizzly bear mount, giving the stuffed pooch a long-snouted, open-mouthed appearance. His wife refused to let it in the house, so he drove it around in his truck.

One day in the 1950s the man was visiting the Shooting Star when he ran up a bar tab that he couldn't pay. So he fetched the stuffed head from his truck and offered it to the owner instead. The dog has since become something of a saloon mascot.

The dollar bills on the ceiling started decades ago when beer cost a quarter. A regular named Whiskey Joe pinned a faded 1901 greenback up there to make sure he always had an emergency cash supply. It's still there, along with many others scribbled with their donors' names and brief stories and covering almost every inch of the ceiling.

The menu's signature item is the Star Burger, which contains two beef patties and two slices of melted cheese sandwiched around a slab of grilled Polish sausage. *USA Today* once pronounced it one of the West's best burgers, and it's not for the faint of heart.

The bar, named in the 1930s by three locals who watched a shooting star streak across the sky from its stoop, is a popular hangout for skiers after a day on the slopes at nearby Snowbasin. You'll find it at 7350 East 200 South near the middle of town (801-745-2002).

Here an Elk, There an Elk, Everywhere an Elk
Hyrum

Unless you're a hunter or a frequent high-country hiker, you probably don't see wild elk very often. But at the Hardware Ranch in a mountain meadow east of Hyrum, you can see hundreds of them all winter long. The big critters are used to people, so maybe they're not that wild anymore. They're still honest-to-goodness Rocky Mountain Elk, though.

The state of Utah established the ranch in 1945 as a way of managing the region's elk herds, which had interfered with farms and ranches that encroached on the animals' historic winter feeding grounds. Wildlife officials began feeding hay to elk at the ranch, and word gradually spread. Once the animals realized they no longer needed to migrate to the valley to graze, they gathered each fall and winter at Hardware Ranch instead for what has become perhaps the world's biggest elk buffet.

The elk eat a lot of hay—two or three tons a day—all of it grown on the 14,400-acre ranch by state wildlife employees. Visitors to the ranch sometimes will see more than 1,500 elk, including cows, calves, and mature bulls with trophy antler racks.

Hardware Ranch is open for wildlife viewing year-round and has a visitor center with elk-education exhibits and programs. The best time to visit, however, is Thursdays through Mondays during the winter, when the ranch offers horse-drawn sleigh rides through the feeding elk herds. The sleds are steered by colorful guides who keep up a steady chatter of elk facts, elk jokes, and other tall tales. (How many elk *does* it take to screw in a light bulb?)

Each October, as the elk begin to gather, the ranch holds an Elk Festival complete with elk bugling contests, decoy-shooting contests, crafts, and presentations by local mountain men.

To reach the ranch, take Highway 101 east from Hyrum about 15 miles until you see the signs. For more info, call (435) 753-6206 or visit www.hardwareranch.com.

Rocks, Funny Money, and a Really Big Hairball

Hyrum

Whoever gathered the items that fill the little Hyrum City Museum had a keen curiosity and a sense of humor. While most small-town Utah museums are filled mostly with pioneer-era artifacts from the area, Hyrum's collection is far-ranging and wonderfully strange.

Sure, you'll see antique tools, a scale model of 19th-century Fort Hyrum, and an inexplicable display on "personal grooming," complete with a mid-1900s "permanent-wave machine."

And you thought cats had big hairballs.

But you'll also find dinosaur eggs from the Gobi Desert, a piece of the Berlin Wall, a bottle of ash from the 1980 Mount St. Helens eruption, a serving tray decorated with hundreds of butterfly wings, a piece of a crashed airplane found in 1953 near the Utah-Idaho border, and a $10 bill from the Salt Lake City National Bank, circa 1874. The museum also has an impressive collection of rocks, crystals, geodes, coral, fool's gold, and petrified wood.

Most curious of all, however, is a gray stone-like orb in a little display case labeled, "hair ball from the stomach of a cow." The thing is the size of a grapefruit. I don't know how it was, um, "collected," or who thought to display it in a museum, but I'm grateful they did.

The Hyrum City Museum is located at 50 West Main Street. For hours and information call (435) 245-6411.

"Happy Days" are Here Again
Layton

If you love vintage cars, *American Graffiti,* and *Happy Days,* then you'll love the Burger Stop, a tasty little slice of 1950s Americana in this Ogden suburb. Posters of Elvis and Marilyn line the walls, the jukebox plays oldies, and in the summertime, classic-car owners from around Northern Utah converge on the parking lot for monthly car shows.

You almost expect the Fonz to strut in, thumbs up, and order a burger.

When owner Travis Theobald opened the Burger Stop in 1993 in a former Hardee's, he wasn't planning on becoming a magnet for lovers of old Corvettes and Mustangs. But they started showing up, and one thing led to another.

Now the place hosts a different-themed "Cruise Night" every month between April and October. For the Beach Bash in July, car owners wear Hawaiian shirts; for the Halloween cruise in October, they dress themselves, and their cars, in spooky costumes. A DJ spins '50s and '60s tunes in the parking lot, and some 150 vintage cars and 2,000 onlookers show up each month.

"It's a pretty big event. We pack the parking lot," Travis says. "That's what kind of separates us from everybody else."

Inside, the restaurant has red-and-white vinyl booths, an antique gas pump, and photos on the walls of customers with their classic rides. The Burger Stop also publishes a popular annual calendar with photos of customers' cars. Oh, and the burgers are pretty good, too.

The Burger Stop is located at 323 East Gentile Street (801-554-8090).

Happy days: Classic cars outside the Burger Stop.

A Grisly Grizzly Tale

Logan

Old Ephraim, Utah's last-known grizzly bear, was large in life—and since his death his ample legend has only grown larger. Ephraim was notorious throughout the Cache Valley in the early 1900s for terrorizing farmers and ranchers by stealing sheep and disappearing into the mountains to devour them. Witnesses say he stood 10 feet tall on his hind legs, weighed more than half a ton, and had only three toes on one foot.

Legend has it he also could bite a 6-inch-thick aspen limb clean through with one chomp. No wonder campers in Ephraim's day shivered in their tents at night.

Old Ephraim met his demise on August 22, 1923, when a sheepherder named Frank Clark was awakened by a roar that starlit night in Logan Canyon east of town. Clark, who had been tracking the bear's movements for twelve years and had set traps around his campsite, went to investigate and found Ephraim with a 14-foot chain wrapped around his right forelimb and a 23-pound bear trap on his paw.

Needless to say, Old Eph was not in a good mood. After Clark fired his gun at him, the bear charged.

"He was coming, still on his hind legs, holding that cussed trap above his head," Clark wrote later. "I was rooted to the earth and let him come within 6 feet of me before I stuck the gun out and pulled the trigger."

It took seven bullets to bring Ephraim down. Clark skinned the bear and buried him where he fell. A few months later a Boy Scout troop dug up the bear's skull and sold it for $25 to the Smithsonian Institution in Washington, D.C., which was eager to document the dwindling grizzly population of the American West.

Although Clark claimed to have seen another grizzly near Logan in 1936, Ephraim became a symbol—the last documented Utahn of his vanishing species. The Smithsonian later loaned Ephraim's skull to Utah State University in Logan, where it remains on display in the campus library.

In 1966 another troop of Boy Scouts dedicated an 11-foot-high stone monument to Old Ephraim beside his gravesite along a trail some 9 miles up Logan Canyon. Engraved on the monument is this poem:

> *Your deeds were so wrong*
> *Yet we built you this marker*
> *And sing you this song*
> *To the King of the forest*
> *So mighty and tall*
> *We salute you, Old Ephraim*
> *The King of them all.*

An Inn for Every Fantasy

Logan

There are bed-and-breakfasts with gently themed rooms, and then there is the Anniversary Inn, which takes fantasy fulfillment to new extremes. The inn is so accommodating to eccentric whims that upon arriving you half expect to be greeted on the lawn by Ricardo Montalban and Tattoo.

The inn's twenty-one rooms and suites include something for almost every taste—from elegance to kitsch, from sophisticated to kiddie playground. Got a thing for King Arthur? No problem. Always wanted to visit an Amazon rain forest? Done.

Options include the "Arctic Journey" room, which is shaped like a snow cave, complete with icicles and statues of penguins; "Lost in Space," which features walls painted like the night sky and a "silver spaceship" bathroom; the "Caribbean Sea Cave" with its underwater-mural walls and double bed inside a boat; and a two-story "Swiss Family Robinson" suite with a treehouse loft, saltwater aquarium, and rock waterfall spilling into a jetted tub.

And I didn't even mention "Aphrodite's Court," "Pyramids of Egypt," "Pirates' Paradise," or the "Jesse James Hideout."

As you can guess, the inn is popular with couples celebrating anniversaries, birthdays, New Year's Eve, or whatever themed holiday you could dream up. There also are two Anniversary Inns in Salt Lake City, but they don't match the Logan location for the sheer variety and creativity of its rooms.

The inn is located at 169 East Center Street. For reservations call (435) 752-3443. For a free peek at all the rooms, visit during the inn's annual open house in early December.

Fill 'er Up With Clover-Alfalfa Please
Logan

Cox Honeyland is to honey what Wisconsin is to cheese. This family-owned honey business offers more honey-related products than you can shake a sweet tooth at: honey candy, honey-covered popcorn, honey almond soap, honey butter and, of course, a dizzying variety of honey itself.

Cox's gift shop, which fills a former two-bedroom house, sells beeswax products, stuffed bears, and the company's many flavored honeys, including orange, cinnamon, apricot, lemon, raspberry, and its most popular variety, huckleberry. That's not counting Cox's creamed varieties, such as almond honey, peanut butter honey, and peach amaretto pecan honey.

Whew! And I always thought honey came in only two varieties: the kind you spread on your toast and what you call your sweetheart when you need something done around the house.

Behind the gift shop is a warehouse where visitors are welcome to fill their own containers with three varieties of Cox honey from 1,000- to 1,500-gallon tanks. Customers are charged by the pound.

Honey has been sweet to the Cox family for four generations now. In 1929, when the rest of the nation was sinking into the Great Depression, Marion Cox began producing honey with a few hives and some bees. Today his son Duane and wife Margene run a year-round honey-producing operation with the help of their two sons, who work as beekeepers, and four daughters, who help out in the warehouse and gift shop.

Honey, bear with me. We're going to Cox Honeyland.

Today Cox honey is sold around the state. In the summertime, Cox honey comes from hives clustered in the fragrant meadows and forests of northern Utah and southern Idaho. During the summer months a working hive even sits inside a revolving display case in the Cox gift shop, where visitors can watch the queen bee lay eggs and the worker bees buzzing in and out through a tunnel to gather nectar from the nearby fields.

You'll find Cox Honeyland at 1780 South Highway 89/91, a few miles south of downtown Logan. For more information call (435) 752-3234 or visit www.coxhoney.com.

Also in Logan:

Gossner Foods, a family-run business that dates to 1941 and was once the largest Swiss-cheese factory in the world. The company sells a variety of cheeses from its retail store at 1051 North 1000 West.

A TOWN IN THE MIDDLE OF A LAKE

For the first half of the 1900s, Utah's most unusual town sat surrounded by water and featured a train track as its only street. Called Midlake, the hamlet sat atop a wooden platform smack dab in the middle of the Great Salt Lake.

Let me explain. Some three decades after the transcontinental railroad was joined on a winding mountain track north of the lake, engineers realized they could save time and money by instead running the trains on a straight line across the inland sea. So from 1902 to 1904, they built a trestle, supported by 38,256 wooden pilings harvested from Western forests, from one side of the lake to the other.

An engineering marvel, the Lucin-Ogden cutoff, as it became known, saved 44 miles and more than twenty-one hours of travel time. Trains crossed the lake day and night, which required workers to maintain the tracks and trestle. So, Midlake was born on a platform 80 feet long by 40 feet wide and suspended 15 feet above the lake.

The town contained a telegraph office, a little store, and a row of houses, some of them converted boxcars. Mail, groceries, and other supplies arrived daily by train. At its peak Midlake had thirty residents, all of them men, who did little but work, eat, and sleep. Liquor was not allowed. Maybe the railroad companies worried that drunk workers might topple off the platform and drown.

The unique town survived for forty-one years until its residents were relocated to the mainland. The aging wooden trestle was replaced in 1959 by a rock-and-earthen causeway on which trains still travel today.

Utah's Stonehenge?
Lucin

OK, so it's not 5,000 years old. Hardly anybody's ever heard of it. And it doesn't attract hordes of tourists, druids, and pagan worshippers. But the Sun Tunnels, a unique sculpture on a remote northwestern desert plain, is maybe the best place in Utah to be during the summer and winter solstices.

New York artist Nancy Holt installed the tunnels—basically four large concrete pipes—in 1976 during a period when artists were experimenting with large-scale sculptural works in nature. Holt probably was influenced by Robert Smithson's Spiral Jetty on the Great Salt Lake, which was built six years earlier. After all, Smithson was her husband.

They don't call them the Sun Tunnels for nothing.

The tunnels' concrete pipes are each 18 feet long and about 8 feet in diameter, allowing visitors to walk upright inside them. They lay on permanent concrete foundations in the shape of an X, with their openings aligned to frame the sun as it rises on June 21 and December 21. Holt pierced each pipe with a cluster of holes that allow the sun to shine through; the shards of interior light shift with the sun over the course of the day. The pattern of holes corresponds to four constellations: Capricorn, Columbia, Draco, and Perseus.

An hour's drive from the nearest town of any size, the Sun Tunnels live a quiet existence. They briefly made news in 2004 when someone listed them for sale on eBay, but the auction turned out to be a hoax. Holt, who now lives in New Mexico, owns the property on which they sit, and she's not selling.

To visit the Sun Tunnels, take Route 30 to Lucin, then head south 2½ miles on a dirt road. Bear left at the first road after the power lines, then head east about 3 miles. The tunnels will be visible on your right.

Over the Rainbow
Ogden.

Rainbow Gardens sounds like a magical kind of place, and in a way, it is. This former hot-springs resort houses a restaurant whose menu has such quirky offerings as an Ahh! Vocado (veggie sandwich), a Gabby Crabby (crab salad sandwich), a Hedda Gobbler (turkey sandwich), and a Mormon Muffin, said to be made from a time-honored pioneer recipe.

But the restaurant pales next to Rainbow Gardens' signature attraction: Its sprawling gift shops. The place bills itself as "Western America's Largest Gift Emporium," and, if you don't count Costco or Wal-Mart, it may be true. The shops are especially festive between September and December, when Christmas decorations fill the shelves and the window displays come alive with live-motion elves and Santas.

The complex's long history dates to the 1890s, when its natural mineral pools attracted bathers drawn to the water's medicinal qualities. Later the place became a Roaring Twenties hotspot whose ballroom hosted dance marathons that sometimes lasted for weeks.

Renamed Rainbow Gardens in 1946, it became a popular recreational spot for Ogden's swimmers, ice skaters, and bowlers (an eighteen-lane bowling alley was added in 1961). The owner of the place was a motorcycle enthusiast who once won a bet by riding his bike down a waterslide into the swimming pool.

As interest in dancing and swimming waned, the owners installed a boutique in the old ballroom and a sunken "gift garden" in the 100,000-gallon pool after it closed in 1972. The restaurant, called the Greenery, followed in 1976, and its decor—a black-and-white tiled floor and leafy trees in barrel planters—probably hasn't changed much since.

Today the cavernous gift shops include more than twenty departments. Be sure to visit Planet Rainbow (located in the former bowling alley), whose eclectic wares include everything from Betty Boop memorabilia to Olympic pins to shot glasses emblazoned with the Salt Lake City Mormon Temple.

You'll find Rainbow Gardens at 1833 Valley Drive, about a mile up Ogden Canyon. For hours and such call (801) 392-3902.

YOU OUGHTA BE IN PICTURES

Mount Ben Lomond, a 9,712-foot peak in the Wasatch Range northeast of Ogden, might look familiar. Its grandeur is believed to have inspired the famous Paramount Pictures logo of the snow-capped peak ringed with stars.

The founder of the movie studio was William Wadsworth Hodkinson, who grew up in Ogden. Legend has it that Hodkinson designed the logo in 1914 after scribbling it on a napkin during a meeting with legendary producer Adolph Zukor. It remains the oldest movie-studio logo in continuous use.

Hodkinson's biographer, Leslie Halliwell, wrote that the Paramount logo was based upon "a memory of childhood in his home state of Utah." While Hodkinson never specified whether an actual mountain inspired his doodling, Ben Lomond is an obvious choice. The grandest of the peaks surrounding Ogden, it dominates the eastern skyline when viewed from the city.

With its pointy top and notched ridgeline, however, the mountain in the logo is more dramatic looking than the actual Ben Lomond, which is named for a peak in Scotland. Leave it to Hollywood to give even a mountain a face lift.

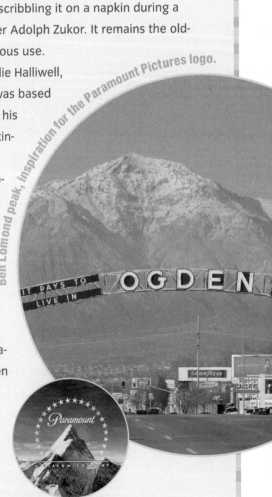

Ben Lomond peak, inspiration for the Paramount Pictures logo.

A Treehouse for Kids

Ogden

It's not called the Treehouse Museum for nothing. This children's museum, which opened in its present location in 2006, has a giant tree growing in the middle of it, from the floor to the roof.

It's not a real tree, but a three-story replica with bark made from a durable compound—the stuff they line pickup trucks with—and some 70,000 silk leaves. The tree's redwood-size trunk is hollow and contains a staircase leading to a platform above the ground. From there, visitors navigate another staircase to the museum's second story.

The tree is home to the museum's mascot, Sam the Squirrel, who makes occasional guest appearances. It also provides a unifying story-book theme and focal point for the museum, which emphasizes interactive educational exhibits—including a miniature Oval Office where kids can play President for a day.

The Treehouse Museum is located at 347 22nd Street (801-394-9663). For security reasons no adults are permitted without accompanying children.

Kids and Grandma alike can climb this treehouse.

Guns, Trains, and Automobiles
Ogden

In its early-to-mid-1900s heyday as a hub for passenger trains crossing the West, Ogden's Union Station was a happening place. Trains don't stop here anymore, but the handsome old depot, built in 1924, has been reborn as a curiosity-seekers' gold mine. What's it got? All this, for starters:

• Two enormous murals on the walls of its main hall by prominent artist Edward Laning, who also painted murals in the New York Public Library and Ellis Island's immigration building. The murals measure 12 by 50 feet each and dramatize the building of the transcontinental railroad. What's strange about them is the way Laning depicted many of the railroad workers: shirtless and rippling with muscles, as if he'd hired Chippendales dancers as models.

This little train, part of the Wattis-Dumke Railroad Exhibit, replicates a 19th-century journey from California to Ogden.

30

- A museum devoted to the famous Ogden-bred Browning family of gun manufacturers, who invented many of the most widely used rifles, pistols, and shotguns in the world. On display are scores of their guns, from an 1894-model Winchester rifle to a Colt .45 pistol to machine guns used by U.S. forces in both world wars. Company founder John M. Browning designed many of them in an Ogden workshop, a replica of which is also on display. Considered by many the greatest firearms inventor in history, Browning is credited with 128 patents; by the time of his death in 1926, those patents had produced more than 50 million sporting and military weapons. The Browning company still maintains its headquarters near Ogden, although many of its guns are now made overseas.
- The Wattis-Dumke Model Railroad Exhibit, arguably the best in the state. There's something about watching a miniature train chug up a mountain, cross a bridge, or emerge from a tunnel that brings out the kid in anyone. But instead of merely circling a fictional scene, these little trains retrace the route of the transcontinental railroad from California to Wyoming. The tracks pass through a series of rooms, each displaying several different historical settings. Kids dash from room to

This vintage car is on display at the Browning-Kimball Car Museum inside Ogden's Union Station.

room, following the trains as they climb the steep grades of the Sierras, navigate the broad Nevada desert, cross a wooden trestle over the Great Salt Lake, and arrive at a miniature scale model of downtown Ogden. Visitors also can watch the trains cross a see-through bridge over a museum corridor.

- The Browning-Kimball Car Museum, which makes up for its size—it contains only ten cars—with automobiles of rare historical vintage. Do you miss the days of running boards, rumble seats, and gleaming chrome fenders? Then these cars are for you. Among the antique luxury models on display are a 1907 Stanley Steamer (yes, it ran on steam); a 1911 Knox whose cousins raced in the inaugural Indy 500; a 1930 maple-interior Cadillac model believed to be the only one of its kind left in the world; and a 1926 Lincoln, once owned by a silent-film star, that squired a young Winston Churchill around Hollywood and appeared onscreen in Charlie Chaplin's *City Lights*. The cars still run and have up-to-date license plates because they're driven each summer in city parades; one, a 1901 Oldsmobile, is considered the oldest registered car in Utah. "All these cars have a story," says volunteer curator Alex Jolin. They sure do.

  Union Station also contains an antique train display, a railroad history museum, a restaurant, an art gallery, and a model-train shop. You'll find the stately building at 2501 Wall Avenue, where a $5 fee gets you into all the museums. It's well worth it. For more information call (801) 393-9886.

The Browning Gun Museum inside Ogden's Union Station.

For Sale: Sixty Acres of Stuff

Ogden

Smith & Edwards has been called "Wal-Mart on anabolic steroids," and it's easy to see why.

First, the sprawling store is surrounded by a sixty-acre junkyard with aisle after aisle of wheels, trailers, pipes, pontoons, hosing, and other industrial scrap—all of it for sale at negotiable prices. Second, its emphasis on guns, hunting, and military surplus supplies gives the store a decidedly macho feel. It's the kind of place Rambo might come to stock up for a rescue mission.

It's like Wal-Mart surrounded by a junkyard.

One of the state's largest and oddest retail businesses, Smith & Edwards has been supplying Utah's hunters and survivalists since 1947. Nicknamed "The Country Boy Store," it's filled with 171,000 square feet of tools, housewares, fishing tackle, camping gear, auto parts, Western wear, beef jerky, guns, ammo, "100% Redneck" bumper stickers, and countless other items. No wonder the store's slogan is "We Have Everything You Want . . . If We Can Find It!"

Among the store's more notable features are a "rope room" with 100-plus varieties; a taxidermy wall with dozens of mounted elks, moose, and other huntable critters; and another section with what seems like an acre of Wrangler jeans. Need a set of steer horns to mount on the grill of your Cadillac? They've got those, too.

Smith & Edward's most colorful section, however, holds its large selection of military surplus gear. Here you can buy several types of parachutes, an array of hollow hand grenades and empty artillery shells, Russian military jackets, a Buckingham Palace guard's uniform, white camo jumpsuits (for wintertime warfare, apparently), and enough green camo clothing to outfit a small army.

Propped up throughout the store are cardboard cutouts of John Wayne in chaps and a cowboy hat, pointing a pistol at anyone who looks his way. Come to think of it, John Wayne would have loved this place.

Smith & Edwards is open every day but Sunday at 3936 North Highway 126, just northwest of Ogden (801-731-1120) and west of I-15. Take exit 351 or 354 off the interstate and follow the signs.

Also in Ogden:

The Millstream Classic Car Collection, an array of vintage automobiles stored at the Millstream motel, 1450 Washington Boulevard. Admission is free, but the cars are shown by appointment only. Call (801) 394-9425.

The George S. Eccles Dinosaur Park, an outdoor attraction along the Ogden River whose grounds are populated with dozens of lifelike dinosaur statues, including some that move. You'll find it at 1544 East Park Boulevard (801-393-3466).

The Coldest Place in Utah

Peter's Sink

I don't know who Peter was, but his sink must be made of ice. That's because this natural sinkhole, 8,000 feet above sea level in the Bear River Mountains east of Logan, routinely produces the state's coldest temperatures.

On February 1, 1985, the temperature here plunged to 69 degrees below zero Fahrenheit—the second-coldest digits ever recorded in the lower forty-eight states. (Ironically, the highest temperature ever recorded in Utah, 117 degrees, came just five months later at the southern end of the state in St. George.)

Scientists believe that temperature inversions trap nocturnal cold air in the sinks, a series of holes in the range that are popular with snowmobilers. The lower you descend into the sinkhole, the colder it gets.

Peter's Sink is so cold that even in the summer, the bottom of the sinkhole never goes four consecutive days without freezing. It's so cold that trees grow at the top of the hole, where it's relatively toasty, but not at the bottom.

If you want to bring your woolies and experience the sink for yourself, head east on Highway 89 up Logan Canyon to the Wasatch-Cache National Forest ranger station, where folks can give you directions. Their number is (435) 755-3620.

But Where's the Spike?

Promontory

As you might remember from high-school history, America's first transcontinental railroad was formed in 1869 when tracks from the East Coast and tracks from the West Coast were joined in remote northern Utah. During a May 10 ceremony a railroad spike made of gold was symbolically tapped and then immediately replaced with an iron spike connecting the two railroads.

Visitors to the Golden Spike National Historic Site today will find a case displaying a golden 4-inch spike inscribed with the names of pioneer-era railroad executives. But before you hop in your car to drive out there and see it, there's something you should know: It's not the spike that was used in the ceremony that day. That spike is 700 miles away at a Stanford University museum in Palo Alto, California.

"THE LAST SPIKE" (a replica)

A replica of the famed Golden Spike used to link the Transcontinental Railroad.

What gives? Well, for starters, the president of the Central Pacific Railroad was Leland Stanford, who later founded the university that bears his name. The contractor who commissioned the golden spike—who also happened to be Stanford's brother-in-law—donated the spike to the university upon its founding in 1892.

Three other ceremonial spikes were used in that 1869 ceremony, and somehow none of them ended up in Utah, either. Stanford also got its mitts on a silver spike, while a spike made from iron, silver, and gold is on display at a museum in New York City. The whereabouts of the third spike, made from laurel wood, are unknown.

The replica spike at the Promontory site does have one claim to fame: It was aboard a Space Shuttle Atlantis flight in 1990 as a symbol of America's first frontier visiting Earth's final frontier.

Visitors to the Golden Spike site can still tour a small museum, watch a twenty-minute historical film and step out back to observe the actual spot where the tracks were joined. Between May 1 and Labor Day, replicas of the two 1869 locomotives sit facing each other on the tracks, and on May 10 of each year, the museum hosts a reenactment of the golden spike ceremony, complete with history buffs in stove-pipe hats.

In case you're wondering, trains don't actually run on the tracks anymore. To save time and money, the railroad companies in 1904 opened a more direct east-west track on a trestle across the Great Salt Lake. The Promontory trains finally stopped running in 1942. In fact, the Promontory site has only about 2 miles of track. If you follow the rails in either direction, they just end, abruptly, in the desert.

To reach the Golden Spike National Historic Site, take Route 83 west from I-15 in Brigham City or Route 102 southwest from I-15 in Tremonton and follow the signs. Admission is $5. And if you want to gripe to someone about the absent spike, the number is (435) 471-2209.

Rockin' Rockets

Promontory

It's a surreal experience to drive along a highway in the middle of nowhere, round a corner, and come face to face with a collection of life-size rockets and missiles pointing into the sky.

Don't worry—we're not getting ready to fire on Iran. It's the Thiokol Rocket Display, and it's an aerospace geek's dream. An outdoor museum of sorts, it's accessible twenty-four hours, just in case you get a strange midnight urge to go look at a missile.

The display sits outside a research and development plant run by Alliant Techsystems (ATK), a weapons and space-systems manufacturer that bought Thiokol in 2001. But everyone still calls it the Thiokol Rocket Display.

Here you'll find full-scale models of many famous rocket boosters and missiles designed by Thiokol

These rockets are a mecca for space geeks.

over the past half-century, all painted white and arrayed on a rocky bed with explanatory labels beside each one. Among the firepower on display are a propellant motor that powers the Patriot anti-aircraft missiles, a 34-foot-long Trident C-4 missile (launched underwater by Trident submarines), and a 59-foot-high Minuteman I ICBM with a range of more than 6,000 miles.

The granddaddy of the display, however, is the reusable rocket motor from the space shuttle. At 149 feet, it's the largest rocket motor ever flown; two of these babies provide 80 percent of the shuttle's thrust during its first two minutes of flight. Recovered boosters like this one are disassembled in Florida and returned to Thiokol in Utah, where they are refurbished for use on future shuttle flights.

The Thiokol Rocket Display is located along Highway 83 about 8 miles northeast of the Golden Spike Historic Site. Access Highway 83 from I-15 in Brigham City and follow the signs.

Hungry for a midnight snack—and a glimpse at a rocket.

MELVIN AND HOWARD

Is Melvin Dummar a scam artist or a Good Samaritan who got royally screwed? We may never know.

You may remember Dummar as the Utah man who claims he saved billionaire Howard Hughes's life after finding him lying in a Nevada desert on a cold winter night. A former gas station operator, Dummar said he was driving December 29, 1967, on Highway 95 when he pulled off onto a dirt road to relieve himself and saw a scraggly man lying face down in the dirt. Dummar helped the man into his Chevy and, at his request, drove him 160 miles to the Dunes hotel in Las Vegas, where he dropped him off.

Dummar said he didn't believe it when the man told him he was Howard Hughes. But after Hughes died in 1976, a handwritten will surfaced that left one-sixteenth of the billionaire's estate—an estimated $156 million—each to Dummar and to his faith, the Church of Jesus Christ of Latter-day Saints.

A Nevada jury tossed out the "Mormon will," as it became known, in 1978 after deciding it was a fake. Dummar never collected a cent. His story made worldwide headlines and spawned a fictionalized 1980 movie, *Melvin and Howard,* directed by Jonathan Demme. It also made him the butt of jokes from people everywhere who thought his story was a ridiculous hoax.

But Dummar's case found new life when a former FBI agent found a former Hughes employee who said he flew his eccentric boss to the Cottontail Ranch brothel—about 7 miles from where Dummar says he found Hughes—over the Christmas holiday in 1967.

In 2006 Dummar filed suit against a Hughes relative and the holding company that controlled Hughes's estate, claiming they conspired to defraud him out of his rightful share of the billionaire's fortune. A Utah court later tossed out the suit.

Melvin, who has worked as a milkman and a country singer and now lives outside Brigham City, says he doesn't care about getting rich—he just wants people to understand that he's not a liar.

"If I had to do it all over again, I'd pick up Mr. Hughes," he says.

Peter and the Jets

Roy

Hill Air Force Base has several unusual distinctions: It's Utah's largest employer. It's named for a World War I–era pilot, Maj. Peter Hill, even though he apparently never set foot in Utah. And its museum boasts one of the largest collections of vintage aircraft in the world.

You can't miss 'em. Located just east of I-15, the Hill Aerospace Museum's grounds are populated with more than a dozen humongous antique planes, from to an 86-foot-long Fairchild "Flying Boxcar" to a 160-foot-long Boeing B-52 bomber called a "Stratofortress." This particular Stratofortress never saw combat, but boy, it sure sounds impressive.

That's not counting another sixty or so aircraft inside two cavernous museum hangars. The first hangar contains displays on the early days of aviation, including a replica of a 1911 Burgess–Wright Bros. Flyer (top speed 42 mph), and a handful of World War II–era fighters with

Huge aircraft populate the grounds of the Hill Aerospace Museum.

such colorful names as "Warhawk," "Invader," and "Jolly Roger." Inside the second hangar are more recent planes and weaponry, including a Minuteman ICBM and some jets capable of sound barrier–busting speeds of 1,500 mph.

The museum lobby has displays on the history of the base, which opened in 1940 as Hill Field and at one time had the busiest runway of any airfield in the free world. More interesting is a room devoted to air-man uniform fashions. It contains mannequins modeling vintage bomber jackets, various types of goggles, and a World War II–era white sheepskin coat, complete with furry Eskimo hood, for Army Air Corps pilots in Alaska.

Don't miss the gift shop, which sells model airplanes, military patches, and freeze-dried astronaut food.

You'll find the Hill Aerospace Museum off I-15's exit 338. The museum is open seven days a week and admission is free. For more info call (801) 777-6868 or visit www.hill.af.mil/museum.

Don't make this vintage fighter plane angry. Oops — too late.

Tell Us Again about the Pioneer Days, Grandpa

Wellsville

Do you chafe at the 21st-century's pampered lifestyle? Do you think kids today are soft and coddled? Are you strangely envious of those pioneer-era western families who bonded together through hardship and misery?

Then the American West Heritage Center is for you. This 160-acre living-history site includes a working historical farm, a pioneer settlement, a mountain-man camp, and a Native American village where visitors can experience firsthand what it was like to live in the west 150 years ago. Think of it as an Old West Disneyland, but with manure and less indoor plumbing.

A pony is among the many farm critters at the American West Heritage Center.

Unlike living-history museums where tourists gawk at employees in period clothes demonstrating how to spin yarn, this center is a hands-on place. Here you can milk a cow, sleep overnight in a teepee, ride in a covered wagon, or pull a handcart for days down a bumpy trail until you've got blisters on top of blisters. Fun!

C'mon everybody, it's time to milk the cow!

The center's most unique offering has to be its handcart treks. Visitors can take a guided trip of up to five days designed to simulate the mid-1800s treks by hardy Mormon pioneers who tugged their belongings across the plains by hand in little wagons. Trips can be customized to include storytelling, whittling, arrow-shooting, and—no, I'm not making this up—"simulated deaths" to convey a sense of the pioneers' sacrifice. I'm not sure whose "deaths" they're talking about.

Although the center is open year-round, most activities are offered during the summer months. The center features a petting zoo, pony rides, Dutch-oven dinners, a cornfield maze (fall only), and mountain-man demonstrations by a fellow named "Two-Eyed Pete." The center also hosts a series of annual heritage festivals, including Historic Weaponry Days each August and "How the West Was Worn" (a clothing festival) in September. Just leave those cell phones at home.

The American West Heritage Center is located along Highways 89 and 91. Its sign is clearly visible from the road. For more information call (435) 245-6050 or visit www.americanwestcenter.org.

THE GHOST OF JEAN BAPTISTE

If you ever visit the Great Salt Lake at night and see a shadowy lone figure or feel a sinister ghostly presence, it might be the specter of Jean Baptiste—possibly Utah's most hated historical figure.

A Salt Lake City gravedigger, Baptiste maintained a quiet existence until 1862, when a young man named Moroni Clawson was shot to death by a police officer while escaping from jail. Since Clawson had no family in Utah, the police buried Clawson in some donated clothes. But when Clawson's brother came to Utah to exhume the body and move it to a family plot, he discovered to his horror that Moroni was naked.

An investigation led to Baptiste's house, where police noticed a stack of boxes in a corner. Upon opening them, they found piles of burial clothing. Further investigation revealed Baptiste had collected clothes, shoes, and personal items by raiding more than 300 graves, including those of children. When officers arrested Baptiste, he was wearing a suit stolen from the grave of a Salt Lake saloon keeper.

When news spread, an angry lynch mob gathered outside the jail where Baptiste was held. Brigham Young himself had to assure residents that their dead loved ones would still ascend to heaven wearing the clothes in which they were originally buried.

Once they realized that Baptiste would likely be murdered in prison, city officials secretly loaded him into a wagon at night, branded his forehead with the words, "grave robber," and transported him to Antelope Island in the Great Salt Lake. Later, fearing he might wade ashore through the shallow water, authorities moved him to the more remote Fremont Island.

But when cattle herders visited Fremont Island three weeks later to check on their animals, Baptiste was nowhere to be found. Wood had been stolen from a ranch house on the island, presumably to build a raft, but Baptiste never turned up in Salt Lake City or anywhere else.

Almost thirty-one years later, hunters found a skeleton with an iron clamp around its leg on the south shore of the lake. Observers speculated the skeleton was Baptiste's until police came forward to say that the convict had no ball and chain on his leg when he was marooned on Fremont Island. The fate of Jean Baptiste remains a mystery today, although some say his ghost still wanders the lake's shoreline.

SALT LAKE VALLEY

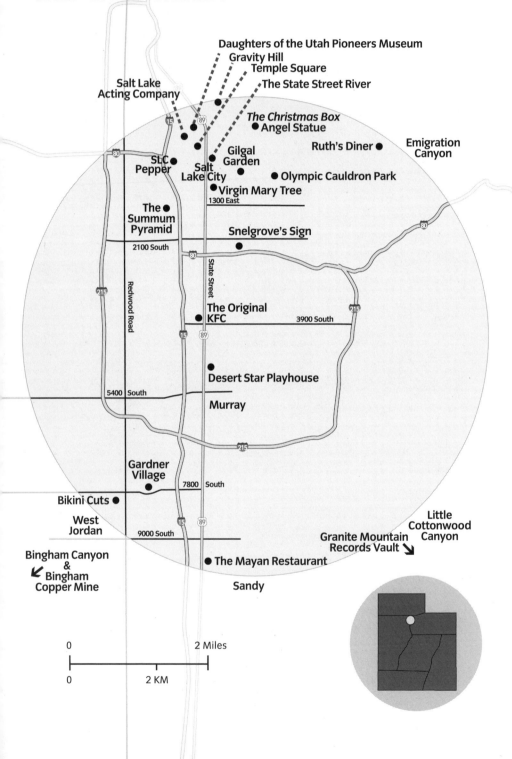

Daughters of the Utah Pioneers Museum
Gravity Hill
Temple Square
The State Street River

Salt Lake
Acting Company

The Christmas Box
Angel Statue

Ruth's Diner ●

Emigration
Canyon

SLC ●
Pepper

Gilgal
Garden

Salt
Lake City

● Olympic Cauldron Park

● Virgin Mary Tree

1300 East

The ●
Summum
Pyramid

2100 South

Snelgrove's Sign

Redwood Road

State Street

The Original
KFC

3900 South

● Desert Star Playhouse

5400 South

Murray

Gardner
Village

7800 South

Bikini Cuts ●

West
Jordan

9000 South

Little
Cottonwood
Canyon

Granite Mountain
Records Vault ↘

Bingham Canyon
↙ &
Bingham
Copper Mine

● The Mayan Restaurant

Sandy

0   2 Miles

0   2 KM

SALT LAKE VALLEY

Sooner or later, everyone passes through Salt Lake City. (Just try flying Delta to Boise, Spokane, or almost any other city in the West without it.) Brigham Young came through town, of course. So did Mark Twain, Karl Malone, Mitt Romney, *Jeopardy!* champ Ken Jennings and, unfortunately, serial killer Ted Bundy, who . . . well, let's just say he was busy while he was here.

And that's not counting the thousands of skiers, skaters, and crooked figure-skating judges who descended on Utah for the Winter Olympics in 2002.

Ringed by mountains on three sides, the Salt Lake Valley is home to more than a dozen municipalities, although most folks here just say they're from Salt Lake. At first glance the valley looks orderly and rather, well, bland. But don't let that fool you. We've got some eccentricities here, starting with the Temple Square area itself, which features a talking Jesus statue and two adjacent residences owned by Brigham Young—one for him and another for some of his twenty-seven wives.

The valley's residents aren't much less colorful today. Salt Lake City mayor Rocky Anderson campaigned for a second term with *Rocky II* stickers and has been known to invite homeless people to sleep in his house. Lee Redmond set a world record with her 30-inch-long fingernails. And the original "Rain Man," Kim Peek, is such a remarkable savant that he can recall some 12,000 books from memory.

The valley's weather can be interesting, too. Recent decades have witnessed a flood that turned a major street into a raging river and a freak tornado that appeared out of nowhere and, for five minutes, turned downtown Salt Lake into Kansas.

So come check out Salt Lake for yourself. You'll discover the world's biggest hole in the ground, a Sphinx statue bearing the face of Mormon Church founder Joseph Smith, a "SLC Pepper" mural by a Utah artist who designed the Beatles' "Sgt. Pepper" album cover, and a pyramid-shaped religious sanctuary where they mummify humans.

Oh, and the first-ever Kentucky Fried Chicken restaurant. In Utah! Go figure.

The World's Richest Hole in the Ground
Bingham Canyon

Near the southwest corner of the Salt Lake Valley you'll find the world's biggest man-made hole—an excavation so massive it's visible from space. Better known as the Bingham Canyon Mine, it's been producing copper for more than a century. So much copper, in fact—plus gold, silver, and molybdenum, a metal used to strengthen steel—that the open pit has yielded more wealth than any other mine on Earth.

Operated by Kennecott Utah Copper Corp., the mine measures 2½ miles across and more than three quarters of a mile deep. That's almost Grand Canyon deep! To give you some perspective, the nation's tallest building, the 1,454-foot-high Sears Tower, would reach only halfway up the mine.

You'll find the world's first open-pit copper mine by taking the 9000 South exit off Interstate 15 and heading west until you hit Route 111, then turning south 4 miles to the entrance. After passing through a security gate, you then climb a winding road past ominous signs warning visitors not to stop. It feels like you're entering some top-secret government facility where they make spy planes or something.

Beyond the parking lot a 100-yard walkway leads you to a fenced overlook, where you can peer down into the pit with the help of 25-cent viewfinders. Because mine crews work around the clock, you'll always see stuff going on. The mine's terraced walls are lined with serpentine roads by which 300-ton capacity trucks haul copper ore to a crushing machine. The crusher squeezes the ore into soccer-ball-size chunks that are then carried on a conveyer belt through a 5-mile tunnel to a processing plant.

The Sears Tower would fit inside this mine, the world's biggest man-made hole.

The terrace at the mine's lip displays mining equipment, most notably a truck tire that is more than 12 feet high and costs $25,000. A nearby visitor center contains educational displays on copper mining and Kennecott's manufacture of gold, silver, and bronze medals for the 2002 Winter Olympics in Salt Lake City. A gift shop sells actual rocks from the mine.

The visitor center is open to the public seven days a week from April 1 to October 31. There is a $5 fee per vehicle. For more information call (801) 252-3234 or visit www.kennecott.com/SD_visitors_center.html.

Burgers, Beer and One Salty Cook

Emigration Canyon

Owner Ruth Evans died in 1989 at the venerable age of 94, but her sharp-tongued spirit lives on at her namesake eatery, Ruth's Diner, in this winding canyon above Salt Lake City. A framed photo by the front door shows Ruth standing before a jukebox while glaring at the camera and cradling a Chihuahua in her arms, a half-smoked cigarette protruding from her lips.

And that was Ruth in a good mood.

Born in the late 1800s, Ruth worked as a cabaret singer before launching Ruth's Hamburgers in 1930 in downtown Salt Lake City. Because the location was across the street from a brothel, many of her regulars were prostitutes who entertained her with stories about their most prominent clients. Ruth was the daughter of a converted Mormon, but considering her two-pack-a-day habit and language that would make a rapper blush, it's safe to say the religion never took with her.

After her building was demolished, Ruth bought an old trolley car in

1946, added a counter and some stools and relocated it three years later to its present spot in Emigration Canyon. Her sign read simply, RUTH'S. HAMBURGERS. BEER. Business boomed.

Since Ruth was rather casual about enforcing liquor laws, her place became especially popular with Utah fraternity boys. She took a similar attitude to the state's new regulations on public smoking; after repeated warnings by the health department, she finally posted a hand-written sign by the door that read, NO SMOKING SECTION— FIRST BARSTOOL ONLY.

Her diners never messed with Ruth.

Ruth finally retired in 1978, when she was 83, and sold the diner to one of her former frat-boy regulars. Today the diner has expanded beyond the original trolley. What used to be Ruth's attached apartment is now the lower dining area, and her former garage is the restaurant's kitchen.

The food has evolved, too. Yep, you can still get meat loaf and chicken-fried steak, but I'm guessing the veggie burger and Thai chicken salad weren't on the menu when Ruth was behind the counter.

One last story: Ruth spent her final years in a duplex behind the diner. When a waitress paid her a visit on her 90th birthday, the gal was shocked to find a pistol between the couch cushions. "Ruth, this gun is loaded!" she cried. Ruth stared back impassively and said, "Well, it wouldn't do me any damn good if it wasn't."

Ruth's is located 3 miles up Emigration Canyon. In the summer, its peaceful back patio is a popular spot for breakfast and lunch. You can call (801) 582-5807 for reservations if you want, but they don't take 'em.

Catacomb of Names
Little Cottonwood Canyon

Some 20 miles southeast of downtown Salt Lake City, buried deep in the rocky foundations of the Wasatch Mountains, is a massive private vault that extends 600 feet into a canyon wall. The main entrance is protected by specially constructed Mosler doors that weigh 14 tons and are stout enough to withstand a nuclear blast.

So what's inside—bars of gold? The Holy Grail? A billionaire mad-man's mountain fortress?

Nope. Genealogical records. Maybe even yours.

The Mormon Church built the Granite Mountain Records Vault, as it's commonly known, in the early 1960s to store the world's largest collection of genealogical material. The climate-controlled vault stores master microfilm copies of census reports, birth records, marriage indexes, death registers, wills, family histories, and other documents, some dating back to the Middle Ages.

That's approximately 2 billion names. The LDS Church uses such information to trace lines of kinship and baptize deceased ancestors of church members. The vault is off-limits to most visitors, but copies of its holdings are available to anyone at the church's Family History Library near Temple Square in downtown Salt Lake City. The library is in the process of transferring its records from microfilm to digital files, which take up much less space and can be accessed globally via the Internet.

Want to preserve your family tree for posterity? The church accepts family histories from anyone, regardless of their religion. Send yours in and the church will make a copy and store it inside the vault, where it'll survive in constant 55-degree temperatures long after you and I are gone.

For more info on the LDS Church's genealogical records, visit www.familysearch.org.

Make 'Em Laugh
Murray

The Desert Star Playhouse will never be confused with a stuffy opera house or a Shakespearean theatre. At least not until Shakespeare is rebooted with pop-culture jokes, audiences encouraged to boo the villain, and cast members who announce patrons' birthdays from the stage.

"We're the theater for people who don't like theater," says managing director Ben Millet. "Our goal is to make people laugh."

This family-friendly playhouse wears its unpretentiousness like a badge of honor. Its original Cabaret Theater has rustic wooden floors, a melodramatic piano player, and a basket of popcorn on every table. It also produces such silly spoofs as "Less Miserable," "My Big Fat Utah Wedding," "The Bi-Polar Express" and "Butch Cassidy and the Sun-burnt Kid."

The playhouse opened in 1989 in a refurbished movie theater. For years the Desert Star also operated a restaurant where patrons who entered wearing a necktie had to remove it or risk having it sliced off and hung from the ceiling. The tie-cutting was done with a large pair of ceremonial scissors and accompanied by the ringing of a bell.

"We didn't just walk right up and whack it off. We basically asked peoples' permission," Millet says. "Because we'd developed this tradition, a lot of people would wear goofy old ties."

One clever customer foiled the tie-cutters by fashioning a necktie from sheet metal. He donated his tie to the ceiling anyway. The restaurant has since been converted to a second dinner theater—hosting Broadway-style musicals—but hundreds of the neckties still hang from the rafters.

You'll find the Desert Star Playhouse at 4861 South State Street. Call (801) 266-2600 or visit www.desertstarplayhouse.com.

Arrgh! There's nothing like a good pirate spoof at the Desert Star Playhouse.

THE REAL "RAIN MAN"

Raymond, the autistic savant played by Dustin Hoffman in *Rain Man,* had a photographic mind, an encyclopedic knowledge of commercial airplane crashes, and some serious blackjack skills.

But that's nothing compared to what Kim Peek, the inspiration for Hoffman's character, can do. Peek, who lives with his father Fran in Salt Lake City, is what's known as a mega savant. Scientists say someone with his astounding mental capacities comes along maybe once in a century.

Peek reads two pages of a book at once and can remember virtually everything he has ever read. If you tell him you were born on February 7, 1949, he'll tell you what day of the week that was. He can recall more than 12,000 books from memory and answer virtually any question about geography, world history, sports, classical music, Shakespeare, the Bible, and a dozen other topics. No wonder his friends call him "Kimputer."

As a boy Kim was diagnosed with mental retardation. He has limited reasoning ability and has trouble performing simple physical tasks, such as tying his shoes. Doctors advised his family to institutionalize him, which Fran Peek refused to do.

In 1984, when Kim was 33, he met screenwriter Barry Morrow, who was so taken by Kim that he used him as a model for his Raymond character in the script he co-wrote for *Rain Man.* Hoffman met with Peek while preparing for the movie.

Peek's life has changed dramatically since the film won the Oscar for Best Picture in 1989. At the urging of Hoffman, Fran Peek decided to share his uniquely talented son with the world. Kim now travels with his father as a motivational speaker, often with Morrow's Oscar, which the screenwriter lets him borrow. Since the movie's release Fran Peek estimates his son has interacted with more than 2 million people.

Wherever he goes, Kim Peek's message is always the same: to respect people's differences. Then he invites audience members to ask him questions on a variety of topics to see if they can stump him. They rarely do.

Come Hear a Choir Sing, a Pin Drop, and Jesus Speak
Salt Lake City

As the worldwide headquarters of the Church of Jesus Christ of Latter-day Saints, Temple Square attracts almost 5 million visitors a year—more than the Grand Canyon—making it Utah's most popular tourist attraction. Because the square is so well known, and a solemn place of worship for more than 13 million Mormons, you might reasonably think there's nothing surprising or odd about it. You would be mistaken!

Sister missionaries, typically clean-cut young women in modest clothing and sensible shoes, lead tours of the square and some of its buildings every ten to fifteen minutes. The tour takes about forty-five minutes and is available in more than forty languages—a testament to the church's vast missionary system, which recruits converts from around the globe. Visiting from Uganda and need a guide who's fluent in Swahili? No problem.

Adam and Eve? Or the leads in "South Pacific"?

SALT LAKE VALLEY

Among the more curious components of Temple Square and its neighboring blocks:

- The Salt Lake Temple itself. The six-spired granite edifice was dedicated in 1893 after forty years of construction. Why so long? Wagons pulled by oxen hauled the granite from Little Cottonwood Canyon, some 20 miles away. As a sacred space, the temple is open only to faithful members of the LDS Church, so its contents are a bit of a mystery to the rest of us. But we know it contains a large baptismal font in which deceased nonbelievers are baptized into the church by proxy. The baptismal font is built atop twelve sculptures of golden oxen, representing not the granite-haulers but the twelve tribes of Israel.

- The Tabernacle. Famous as home to the Mormon Tabernacle Choir (or the MoTabs, for short), the oval-shaped hall contains an organ with 11,623 pipes, making it one of the largest in the world. The Tabernacle (not to be confused with the Tavernacle, a bar five blocks away) also is known for its near-perfect acoustics. Tour guides drop pins or tear newspaper pages on the pulpit to demonstrate how the sound can be heard clearly throughout the hall (so think twice about whispering anything in here). If you visit on Thursday evenings, you can hear the MoTabs rehearse.

- The *Christus* statue. The square's north visitor center features a domed room containing an 11-foot white statue of Jesus Christ against a huge blue mural of the universe dotted with stars and planets. Visitors are instructed to sit before Jesus, whose arms are outstretched in blessing and who speaks in soothing recorded tones (in multiple languages, of course), "Behold. I am Jesus Christ. I created the Heavens and the Earth . . . " Jesus is a hard act to follow, so he usually comes near the end of the tour.

- The LDS Conference Center. Completed in 2000, this terraced granite building has hundreds of live trees growing on its roof and a 67-foot waterfall that spills down its south face. Its cavernous main hall holds 21,200 people, making it the largest religious auditorium in the country.

- The Beehive and Lion houses. These historic homes are best known as official residences of church leader Brigham Young. The 1854 Beehive House, named for a beehive sculpture on its roof, offers public tours by guides who'll tell you that Young lived here with wife Lucy and their seven children. What they don't tell you is that the adjacent Lion House was built two years later to accommodate many of his twenty-six other official wives (unofficially, the tally is closer to fifty wives) and their kids. In the summer months the grounds contain a Young Women Values Garden consisting of seven planters, each blooming with flowers of a different color to represent such "young women" values as faith (white), integrity (purple), knowledge (green), and so on. There's no such garden for the church's Young Men, who are on their own, apparently.

A talking Jesus Christ — how cool is that?

On the second floor of the North Visitors Cer[...] togenic young man and woman dressed in what [...] wear. The man is gesturing grandly with one har[...] painted on the wall, is a mural of a tropical para[...] of an Old Testament display, is supposed to depict Adam and Eve in the Garden of Eden. But let's be honest here: It looks more like a scene from "South Pacific."

A block-and-a-half to the east of Temple Square, on First Avenue between State and A streets, lies Brigham Young's grave. The grave sits in the southeast corner of a handsome little park. But the former Mormon Church leader is not resting alone. To the north of him, laid out in a row, are the graves of four of his wives.

For more information on Temple Square visit www.lds.org/placesto visit and click on Salt Lake City.

Brigham Young is buried here next to four of his wives.

Everything but the Pioneers' Kitchen Sink, and Maybe That, Too

Salt Lake City

Don't be put off by the Pioneer Memorial Museum's official-sounding title or staid façade. Enter this three-story building on Salt Lake City's Capitol Hill and you'll find a trove of oddball stuff, including antique dolls carved from avocado pits and a two-headed stuffed lamb.

The museum bills itself as "the world's largest collection of artifacts on one particular subject," and it's hard to argue the claim. The musty rooms contain display case after display case crammed with items used by the Mormon pioneers who settled Utah in the mid-1800s.

Many of the items were hauled almost 2,000 miles across the plains on wagons and in handcarts. The linens and teapots should have been easy to carry on the arduous trek to Utah, but you can almost hear the griping that must have accompanied the antique piano.

The displays offer little explanatory text—just thousands of pioneer quilts, china, eyeglasses, knives, clocks, bonnets, saddles, guns, clothes, toys, cradles, furniture, musical instruments, and anything else you can think of. Gazing upon this smorgasbord from the walls are rows upon rows of solemn portraits of 19th-century pioneers.

Among the stranger artifacts on view: a lock of LDS Church founder Joseph Smith's hair, a scale model of a Utah sugar factory made entirely from sugar, and a table crafted from more than 100,000 tiny pieces of wood obtained from forty-eight states and seventeen countries.

Visitors also will find a room filled with dolls of all shapes and styles, including some whose faces are carved from peach pits, walnuts, potatoes, and apples. Needless to say, the 150-year-old apple dolls look a little wizened.

A tunnel from the museum's basement leads to the Carriage House, where you'll encounter a horse-drawn surrey, described in the museum guide as "the surrey with the fringe on top." (Is it just me, or shouldn't that surrey be in *Oklahoma's* pioneer museum?) Also in the Carriage House is a wooden, outhouse-like structure, informally known as "Brigham's sauna," that was used by pioneer leader Brigham Young for his steam baths.

The museum is run by the Daughters of Utah Pioneers, a historical preservation group. It's located at 300 North Main Street, just southwest of the state Capitol. Admission is free. For more information call (801) 532-6479.

This two-headed lamb is one of many odd items at the Daughters of Utah Pioneers museum.

For The Birds

Salt Lake City

Considering Utah's status as a landlocked state some 800 miles from the nearest ocean, its official state bird sounds like some sort of joke. It's the seagull. No kidding. (No doubt somewhere a gull-filled coastal state is still resentful about this.)

Why the seagull, you might rightly ask? Well, they nest along the Great Salt Lake. But the real reason is this: According to Mormon legend, the pioneers who settled the Salt Lake Valley in the summer of 1847 were a hardy group who nonetheless almost starved during the bitter winter that followed. So in the spring of 1848 the pioneer colonists planted extensive crops. Just as the crops were ripening, however, hordes of voracious crickets from the nearby foothills descended on the fields and began to devour the fruit of the settlers' labors.

The pioneers battled them as best they could, but their winter food supply seemed doomed. Then, as if summoned from the heavens, a huge flock of seagulls swooped in from the Great Salt Lake and gobbled up the crickets, saving many of the crops.

So near the southwest corner of Temple Square stands a monument commemorating this "modern-day miracle." Designed by sculptor Mahonri Young, a grandson of Brigham Young, it depicts two gold-plated seagulls atop a 20-foot column ringed by a fountain. Tourists toss coins into the water, as if offering thanks to the winged saviors above.

Because the cricket-seagull saga was barely mentioned in historical accounts of the time, some Mormon scholars believe the tale is all feathers. But it makes for a good story—and an unlikely Utah state bird.

Chicken Pete
Salt Lake City

Want to stump your friends at trivia? Ask them the location of the first Kentucky Fried Chicken restaurant. Against all logic, it's in Utah—and still operating on the same spot.

The unlikely story goes like this: Harlan Sanders first sold his fried chicken during the Depression, out of a gas station he owned in Corbin, Kentucky. When the interstate highway system was built after World War II, Sanders hit the road in search of restaurants that would serve his eleven-herbs-and-spices recipe while giving him 5 cents for each piece of chicken sold. The first person to take him up on his offer was Leon W. "Pete" Harman, a Salt Lake City burger-joint operator who began serving the Colonel's chicken at his Harman's Café in 1952.

The first Kentucky Fried Chicken franchise? It's not in Kentucky.

As you might guess, it was an immediate hit. "We couldn't cook the chicken fast enough," Harman said. Although Colonel Sanders pioneered the famous secret recipe, Harman created the "bucket o' chicken" concept that has defined the chain's takeout service ever since. The first KFC buckets, sold at Harman's in 1957, contained fourteen pieces of chicken, five rolls, and a pint of gravy. Price? $3.50.

Harman's KFC contains a mini-museum, complete with one of the Colonel's famed white suits.

Thanks to this successful partnership, Harman became vice president of KFC in 1964 and eight years later was "Colonel-ized" by the state of Kentucky—the bluegrass equivalent of being knighted in England.

Unfortunately the original KFC was renovated in 2004 to look, at least from the outside, like almost every other KFC in the world. But the towering HARMAN'S CAFE sign still stands outside, and an outdoor dining patio contains life-size bronze statues of Sanders and Harman.

Inside, the restaurant doubles as a museum of KFC lore. Walls and tables are filled with historical photos and factoids. Glass cases display an original chicken pressure cooker, one of the Colonel's white suits, and his trademark black string tie. According to the accompanying text, Sanders favored the string tie because "it goes with almost everything and it never drags on a soiled table while you are cleaning up after customers."

Besides chicken, the restaurant sells souvenir T-shirts, baseball caps, aprons, coffee mugs and, yes, even black string ties. You'll find the world's first KFC on one of Salt Lake's busiest commercial corridors at 3890 South State Street (801-266-4431).

HELLO, JELL-O!

Step into the House of Representatives chamber at the Utah Capitol and you'll see a grandly impressive room appropriate to the passing of significant laws. But in 2001 the assembled legislators voted overwhelmingly for a much less serious measure: a resolution recognizing Jell-O as "a favorite snack food of Utah."

Yes, Jell-O. Utahns are famous for their sweet tooth, and the state's residents have for years been the leading per-capita consumers of the jiggly stuff. Jell-O gelatin recipes with fruit, nuts, and marshmallows turn up at almost every Utah church and community dinner.

When Iowa briefly edged out Utah in 1999 as the capital of Jell-O consumption, it was front-page news in stunned Salt Lake City. Encouraged to "Take Back the Title," Utahns bellied up to the dessert table and did just that.

So on January 31, 2001, Utah lawmakers welcomed a special guest to their chambers: longtime Jell-O pitchman Bill Cosby, who helped them commemorate their state's affection for the candy-colored dessert. Cosby passed out autographed boxes of Jell-O and cracked jokes before legislators and then-Gov. Olene Walker, all of whom giggled like schoolchildren at his antics.

"Somebody must have put caffeine in your Jell-O," the comedian quipped.

The Jell-O resolution was the result of a petition drive by Brigham Young University students who gathered almost 15,000 signatures requesting that the dessert be named the official state snack. Its status was further cemented the next year when a 2002 Winter Olympics pin, designed to celebrate the Games in Salt Lake City, featured a bowl of green Jell-O. It became a valuable collectors' item.

The State Street River

Salt Lake City

Stand along State Street at about 100 South and you'd never imagine the busy downtown thoroughfare had a brief life as a raging river. But it did, in the soggy spring of 1983, when floodwaters ravaged Salt Lake City and twenty-one of Utah's twenty-nine counties qualified for federal disaster relief.

Blame a late-May heat wave and melting snow for the flood, which caused City Creek to overflow its banks in the foothills just north of downtown. On normal days the creek flows south out of City Creek Canyon and is diverted underground at North Temple, where it then flows west under the asphalt to the Jordan River.

In 1983, a flood turned this downtown street into a river.

But on May 28 of that year, the swollen creek leaped its shallow banks, lapped against downtown office buildings, and then roared south down State Street, just east of Temple Square. Volunteers with sandbags rushed to harness the sudden river, which flowed to 1300 South before joining other floodwaters and heading west.

Thanks to thousands of volunteers mobilized by the LDS Church, the State Street River was contained with walls of sandbags, preventing millions of dollars in property damage. Workers built temporary wooden pedestrian bridges over the river, allowing downtown office workers to go about their business. Then-Gov. Scott Matheson told the national media, "This is a helluva way to run a desert."

The muddy river flowed through the heart of the city for almost two weeks. Nearby restaurants and shops exploited the novelty, as tourists came from all over to see the bizarre sight and stroll along its banks. One man tossed a fishing line into the stream and caught a trout; his feat was captured in a photograph in *The Salt Lake Tribune*.

The river reverted to its normal course on June 11, although the cleanup effort lasted several more weeks. It was such a popular attraction that some residents urged officials to bring City Creek above ground permanently and incorporate its waters into the design of the city. The advice was ignored, and the State Street River dried up for good.

But those who saw it say they'll never forget.

Gravity Hill

Salt Lake City

Maybe a better name for this weird spot would be Anti-Gravity Hill.
me explain: A gravity hill is defined as a place where the topography o
the land produces the optical illusion that a slight downhill slope
appears to be an uphill slope. Or vice versa.

In Salt Lake City, Gravity Hill is actually a one-way road, Bonneville
Boulevard, which loops through City Creek Canyon, northeast of the
state Capitol, from east to west. Driving the road produces a paranormal effect that you're going downhill when in fact you are gaining elevation. They say if you stop at what appears to be the bottom of the hill
and put your car in neutral, your car will actually coast back "up the
hill."

Of course, people are rumored to be buried in secret graves in the
area, too, so who knows what's really causing this effect. So go on and
give it a try for yourself—just make sure nobody is behind you when
you do.

SLC Pepper
Salt Lake City

Adorning the east wall of a three-story parking garage along 400 West downtown is a large mural populated, collage style, with dozens of famous faces. Called *SLC Pepper,* the public artwork is a 21st-century take on the Beatles' iconic "Sgt. Pepper" album, arguably the most influential record in rock 'n' roll history.

Jann Haworth, the Utahn behind the *SLC Pepper* project, is uniquely qualified to update the classic Beatles record art. In 1967 Haworth, then a budding British artist, helped design the album's original artwork.

Haworth's then-husband, Peter Blake, was the lead art designer for "Sgt. Pepper and the Lonely Hearts Club Band." Haworth hand-tinted black-and-white photos for the cover and created the cloth figures along its right border. For their efforts, she and Blake both won Grammys.

Jann Haworth is uniquely qualified to create this Beatles tribute. She worked on the original "Sgt. Pepper" cover.

After moving in 1997 to Utah, where she ran art programs at Robert Redford's Sundance resort, Haworth decided it would be fun to revisit her most famous project. She was bothered by the fact that of the original cover's seventy-one heads, only seven are women, and all but four are white.

So Haworth surveyed Utahns about which contemporary or historical figures should be on the mural, then rounded up thirty volunteer artists to help her paint it. Most of the mural was completed in 2004, although artists are still making additions.

Gone are the original cover's head shots of Karl Marx, Bob Dylan, Oscar Wilde, and Mae West, plus the gurus added at the request of George Harrison. In their place are novelist singer Bjork, labor leader Cesar Chavez, rocker Jimi Hendrix, and artist Frida Kahlo.

Haworth hopes to add life-size steel cutouts of the four marching-band outfits the Beatles wear on the album cover. The cutouts will be built on a platform several feet in front of the mural, allowing visitors to pose behind them—become the Beatles! Eventually, Haworth hopes to add a sound system that will play Beatles' songs. With a little help from her friends, of course.

You'll find *SLC Pepper* on 400 West between 200 and 300 South.

WHAT'S WITH ALL THE NUMBERED STREETS?

Many first-time visitors to Salt Lake City express bewilderment at its numbered street system, which produces addresses like 525 North 300 West or 1300 East 10600 South.

If you're confused blame LDS Church founder Joseph Smith, who decreed that all Mormon settlements should be laid out in a numbered grid with the temple in the center. Brigham Young, following the recently slain Smith's wishes, established the street system in Utah shortly after founding Salt Lake City in 1847.

The focal point for the city's street grid is the southeast corner of Temple Square. Streets extend in ascending numerical order from the square: 100 South, 200 South, and so on, sort of like latitude and longitude lines on a map. This means that no matter where you are in the Salt Lake Valley, you'll always know about how many blocks you are from the Salt Lake Temple. Streets with actual names (yes, Salt Lake has those, too) always include the numerical coordinates on their signs.

Once you figure it out, the system actually makes a lot of sense. Mormon pioneers quickly established a similar numbered street grid in every Utah town they settled in the 1800s. You can always tell the towns that weren't founded by Mormons, like Park City, because their street-naming system is different.

More than the Summum Their Parts

Salt Lake City

If you visit a modest residential neighborhood west of downtown Salt Lake City and come across a 26-foot-high copper pyramid, don't be alarmed. That's just the sanctuary and world headquarters of the Summum religion and philosophy—one of the oddest faiths you'll ever encounter.

A shrine to Egypt? Not quite. It's the world headquarters of the Summum religion.

That is, unless you don't see anything strange about twelve-hour orgasms as a means to spiritual ecstasy, drinking alcoholic nectars before meditating, and mummifying pets and humans after death. And people think Mormons are eccentric?

Summum was founded in 1975 by Claude Nowell, a Salt Lake City businessman who left the LDS Church, and his wife, after beginning a daily practice of meditation that she didn't understand. While meditating one night in October of that year, Nowell says he heard an intense, high-energy frequency and opened his eyes to discover "Summa individuals" before him who began to plant information inside his head.

These beings began appearing to him regularly during his meditations, teaching him concepts on which he established the religion. Nowell, who changed his name in 1980 to Summum Bonum Amen "Corky" Ra, built the pyramid in 1979, and spread the tenets of Summum philosophy to anyone who would listen. Followers claim to have seen him cry tears of blood, turn a blue sky into a rainstorm, and light a candle just by looking at it.

Corky, as he's commonly known, now claims 200,000 Summum members worldwide. The Summum philosophy borrows from many cultures and religions, but most of its teachings come from ancient Egypt—thus the pyramid, which serves as a symbolic womb of creation.

Inside the pyramid Summum members produce divine nectars used in meditation ceremonies; because the nectars contain alcohol, the state of Utah forced church members to obtain a winery license. A key meditation revolves around sexual ecstasy. But the most curious Summum practice is its emphasis on mummification, which members believe creates a reference point for the soul.

Several mummified dogs and cats sit inside the Summum pyramid, and for a fee the church offers mummification to anyone who wants their remains preserved for posterity. To date more than 1,400 people worldwide have reportedly paid Summum in advance to have their bodies mummified. Summum claims to be the only organization in the world today offering this service.

Still curious? The Summum pyramid, at 707 Genesee Avenue, offers public philosophy classes every Thursday at 7:30 p.m. For more info, or to look into mummifying your pet poodle, visit www.summum.us.

The Weeping Virgin Tree
Salt Lake City

No doubt you've heard stories about images of the Virgin Mary appearing spontaneously on walls, windows, and slices of toast. Well, Salt Lake City has a Virgin Mary sighting of its own, in an elm tree just south of downtown.

In 1997 someone discovered an image of what appeared to be a robed figure in a sawed-off branch of a tree in a small city park on 700 South. Sap oozed from the head of the figure, as if she was crying. Word quickly spread, and people set a ladder against the tree for better access to the "Weeping Virgin" some 9 feet above the ground.

Because the ladder allowed only one person to see the image at a time, the city built a permanent staircase to a small wooden viewing platform. Worshippers tacked dozens of images of Mary and Jesus to the platform, hung rosary beads, kissed the wooden image, and left flowers. The site became especially popular with members of Salt Lake's Catholic Latino population, and the benches beside the makeshift shrine groaned under scores of votive candles.

Unfortunately, vandals chopped out the apparition in 2002, leaving only a jagged hole. News of the desecration spread quickly through the city's Hispanic community, and mourners flocked to the tree. Nobody was ever charged with the crime.

But a curious thing happened. Despite the damage, the site continues to attract a steady stream of believers. The candles still flicker, and the faithful continue to leave behind snapshots of their loved ones—preserving this spontaneous Catholic shrine in the heart of predominantly Mormon Utah. The Virgin Mary tree stands on the north side of 700 South between 200 and 300 East.

Believers lined up to see an image of the Virgin Mary in this tree.

Gilgal Garden

Salt Lake City

Hidden behind homes in the center of a leafy residential block east of downtown is one of the odder sculpture gardens you'll ever see. That is, unless you've been to other parks that contain a statue of a man wearing brick pants, or a miniature Sphinx adorned with the face of Mormon Church founder Joseph Smith.

Unlike most public sculpture gardens, which are planned as civic art projects, Gilgal arose organically from the private backyard obses-sion of a guy with no formal art training. He was Thomas B. Child Jr., a stonemason and devout Mormon who clearly knew a thing or two about carving rocks.

Now, that's a fine pair of brick pants.

Child began working on his garden in 1945, when he was 57. The project consumed the remaining eighteen years of his life and may have provoked some "he's got rocks for brains" comments from his neighbors before the full scope of his vision was realized.

Haven't you ever seen a Sphinx with Joseph Smith's face before?

Named for a biblical settlement along the River Jordan, Gilgal is a monument to Child's religious beliefs. The garden features twelve original sculptures, arranged in a rough circle, and more than seventy stones inscribed with poems, scriptures, and philosophical texts. (Gilgal means "circle of stones" in the Old Testament.)

To build his garden Child traveled Utah in search of huge stones, some the size of VW Beetles, which he wrestled back to his yard through extraordinary means. One 32-ton boulder was hauled in a sixteen-wheel truck to the garden, where Child tipped it from a scaffold onto a specially built concrete foundation. He also used a torch to cut and shape the rocks.

The garden's most famous sculpture, the Smith Sphinx, represents Child's belief that the answers to life's mysteries can only be discovered through faith, not intellect. Another quirky sculpture shows Child, a Bible under one arm and blueprints under the other, wearing pants made from bricks and a stone sport coat.

"I know it is egotistical," Child said of this self-portrait, "but in my travels, which include Europe, I have never seen a better looking or more interesting coat."

After Child's death, Gilgal Garden remained a semisecret place for decades. While neighbors would wander among its stones, many Utahns didn't even know it was there. By the 1990s years of neglect had left the garden in poor shape, and its landowners were considering an offer from a condo developer.

But a group of private citizens and artists led a successful campaign to restore the garden. It was preserved in 2000 as a Salt Lake City park, bestowing official status on Child's quirky personal project. The entrance to the garden is located on 500 South at 749 East. For more information, visit www.gilgalgarden.org.

HOLY TORNADO!

We've all seen *Twister*, and tornadoes occur in Midwestern states such as Kansas and Oklahoma. They don't occur in Utah. At least that's what people in Salt Lake City thought until a freak funnel cloud ripped without warning through the city's downtown on August 11, 1999, killing a man, uprooting more than 800 trees, and causing some $170 million in property damage.

The rare tornado carried winds of up to 156 mph and produced hail the size of marbles. It was the first storm of such magnitude in Utah in thirty-one years.

No warning was issued, because the tornado formed so swiftly that it didn't show up on the National Weather Service's radar. The weather above Salt Lake was clear, sunny, and calm until shortly before 1:00 p.m., when the skies turned a bizarre dark green and winds started swirling. Even then, witnesses weren't too worried until the storm shattered windows in the Wyndham hotel, toppled a construction crane, and peeled off part of the roof of the Delta Center, home of the Utah Jazz.

A visitor from Las Vegas became the first person killed by a tornado in state history when flying debris struck him in the head.

The funnel cloud touched down just west of downtown, then cut a narrow swath across Temple Square, Capitol Hill, and the Avenues neighborhood before dissipating in the foothills to the northeast. Mormons noted that despite the rampant destruction, the Salt Lake Temple was untouched.

Ten minutes after the storm departed, the skies were clear again. The only remaining evidence of its destruction is in denuded Memory Grove Park, where hundreds of large trees were toppled and later removed. That, and the stories Salt Lake City folks still tell of the freak Tornado of 1999.

Thirty Years of Voyeurs
Salt Lake City

What do you get when you combine political satire, silly songs, jokes about Mormons, and lots and lots of booze? *Saturday's Voyeur,* a musical parody that's the longest-running theatrical production in the state.

The show's title is a play on *Saturday's Warrior,* a popular Mormon musical about a young man who leaves home to become a rock star. Its first edition was written by a non-Mormon, Nancy Borgenicht, and an ex-Mormon, Michael Buttars, to lampoon quirkier aspects of Utah's religious culture, such as tie-wearing missionaries, "swears" of "Oh my heck!" and Mormons' peculiar passion for green Jell-O.

Some Mormons considered the show mean-spirited, but it struck a chord with other Utahns frustrated by the pervasiveness of LDS culture. Songs like "Salt Lake, Salt Lake" were sung to the tune of "New York, New York" and brought down the house with lines like, "If I can live out here, I can live anywhere."

After premiering in 1978 at a Unitarian Church, the show moved to the Salt Lake Acting Company, a left-leaning theater located in, of all things, a former Mormon church. *Voyeur* has been staged there every summer since, drawing laughs with lines like, "What's the difference between LSD and LDS? One you take with a cube of sugar, the other with a grain of salt."

Adding to the revelry is the theater's cabaret-style seating, which encourages patrons to bring in their own food and liquor. Many do.

In the mid-1990s Borgenicht and new co-writer Allen Nevins began rewriting the show from scratch each spring to spoof topical events from the past year. Recent *Voyeurs* have poked fun at the Salt Lake Olympics bribery scandal, the Bush Administration's foibles, and a Utah movie-theater owner's decision to ban *Brokeback Mountain*.

Saturday's Voyeur runs every year from mid-June through the end of August at the Salt Lake Acting Company, 168 West 500 North. The show has become so popular that it's the theater's chief source of income. For more information call (801) 363-SLAC or visit www.saltlake actingcompany.org.

Our Little Angel Statue
Salt Lake City

In 1993 a Salt Lake City ad executive named Richard Paul Evans self-published *The Christmas Box,* a sentimental little tale about a young Utah couple who agree to care for a lonely old widow during the holidays. The book eventually became the first ever to top both the hardcover and paperback best-seller lists simultaneously, sold eight million copies, and was made into a TV movie.

In the book, the widow mourns the loss of a child at the base of an angel monument. Evans believes such a statue did once exist in Salt Lake but has disappeared. So after hearing reports that grieving readers were seeking out the angel, Evans commissioned a new statue and erected it in the Salt Lake City Cemetery, near where his fictional story takes place.

The bronze statue was modeled according to Evans's description in his book, and its face is that of Allyson-Danica, Evans's second daughter. Inscribed on its pedestal is the phrase, "Our Little Angel." At a December 6, 1994, dedication ceremony—corresponding with the date of the child's death in the book—Evans encouraged grieving parents to visit the statue and leave flowers.

Every December 6, the statue hosts a candlelight "healing ceremony." And more than a decade after Evans's book faded from the bestseller lists, visitors still leave roses, photos, cards, and mementos. *The Christ-*

mas Box has also inspired more than twenty-five other angel statues across the country—although the Salt Lake City statue was the first.

As far as we know, it's the world's only angel statue inspired by a fictional angel statue that was inspired by real angel statue. You'll find the *Christmas Box*–inspired angel statue just west of Center Street in the middle of the Salt Lake City Cemetery, 200 North Street in the city's Avenues neighborhood. The cemetery is open daily from 8:00 a.m. until dusk.

Fans of Richard Paul Evans's *The Christmas Box* visit this angel statue each December.

An Arch, a Cauldron, and Seventeen Days of Memories
Salt Lake City

The Doors' Jim Morrison would have loved the slogan for the 2002 Winter Olympics in Salt Lake City, which was, "Light the Fire Within." (I can hear it now: "Baby you can light the fire. . .") The slogan applied both to the competitive spirit that burns within each athlete and to the ceremonial lighting of the Olympic cauldron, one of the highlights of every Games.

In Salt Lake City that fire was lit on February 8, 2002, by members of the United States' 1980 gold-medal hockey team, during opening ceremonies at Rice-Eccles Stadium. No flame burns in the 117-foot-tall torch today, but you can still view the striking, glass-and-steel tower at the Olympic Cauldron Park—the place to go for anyone looking to relive the 2002 Games.

Also at the park is the Hoberman Arch, a spiraling curtain of steel designed by inventor Chuck Hoberman, best known for his folding toy spheres. The arch opens and closes like the iris of an eye, or a camera lens, and was the centerpiece of the 2002 Olympic Medals Plaza, where winning athletes received their hardware and rocked out to concerts by Barenaked Ladies and 'NSYNC.

The park sits just south of the University of Utah's football stadium, where the opening and closing ceremonies were held. It also features a small museum with 2002 competition photos, portraits of the athletes, and a short film on the seventeen days of the Salt Lake City Games. Admission is free, but adults must pay $3 to see the movie.

While the cauldron's flames are hardy enough to withstand 100 mph winds, you probably won't see them. The cauldron was relit during the 2006 Torino Games but was apparently not designed to burn more than a few times. Plus it costs tens of thousands of dollars to light the thing. So like Picabo Street, it's pretty much retired.

Olympics fans will find the park on 500 South at about 1500 East. For more info visit www.saltlake2002.com.

TRENT HARRIS, OFFBEAT FILMMAKER

Nobody will ever confuse Trent Harris with Ron Howard or Steven Spielberg. Harris lives in Salt Lake City, not La-La Land. His cult movies are seen by thousands, not millions. And the subject matter of his films is a little, well, odd. Take 1991's *Rubin and Ed,* in which Crispin Glover and Howard Hesseman wander the Utah desert looking for a proper place to bury a frozen cat.

Harris followed that movie with *Plan 10 From Outer Space,* which in typical quirky Harris fashion, has no connection whatsoever to the 1959 Ed Wood–directed *Plan 9 From Outer Space.* Like *Plan 9,* however, Harris's *Plan 10* is a campy low-budget affair about humans trying to foil an evil alien plot, or something. Karen Black (*Nashville*) has a supporting role as an alien queen.

Then came *Beaver Trilogy,* Harris's strangest film and a project that actually stemmed from the early days of his career. It began in 1979 with a chance encounter in a Salt Lake City parking lot between Harris, then a TV news cameraman, and "Groovin' Gary," a young misfit from Beaver, Utah. Gary persuaded Harris to film him in drag, impersonating Olivia Newton-John at a Beaver talent show.

Fascinated with Gary's struggles for acceptance, Harris shot some improvised footage in L.A. in 1981, this time with a then-unknown Sean Penn as Gary. Four years later Harris recruited Glover, who had just filmed *Back to the Future,* to play Gary in a thirty-five-minute film he called *The Orkly Kid.*

Beaver Trilogy features footage from all three versions, edited into a bizarre and poignant triptych of one outcast's small-town dreams. It has screened at New York's Lincoln Center and at the 2001 Sundance Film Festival and has received widespread press as a cult-film curiosity.

Sean Penn has probably left it off his resume, though.

Ice Cream, You Scream, We All Scream: Where the @#% is It?

Salt Lake City

Drive along 2100 South on the east side of Salt Lake City and you'll see a large freestanding sign for Snelgrove Ice Cream. Atop the sign is a huge revolving double cone with chocolate and vanilla scoops. Underneath the Snelgrove, in smaller letters, is a boastful slogan: THIS IS AMERICA'S FINEST ICE CREAM STORE.

Wow, you think, your mouth beginning to water. *How can I not stop for America's finest ice cream store?*

So you pull over and begin looking around, only to realize: There's no store here, just a manufacturing plant and distribution center with Dreyer's Grand Ice Cream trucks parked outside. What gives?

This taunting sign is all that's left of one of Utah's most beloved ice cream parlors.

Turns out there was a Snelgrove's ice cream parlor on this spot, but it closed in 2002 to make more room for California-based Dreyer's, its parent company. That's a shame, because Snelgrove's was a classic. Founded in 1929 by C. R. and Fidella Snelgrove, the family-run business soon became famous.

Legend has it that Franklin Roosevelt had Snelgrove's ice cream flown to the White House in 1935 for Thanksgiving dessert. Some fifty years later, when the Utah Jazz met the Michael Jordan–led Chicago Bulls in the 1997 NBA Finals, Salt Lake City Mayor Dee Dee Corradini offered Snelgrove's ice cream in a ceremonial bet with the Chicago mayor. She lost, of course.

With its red vinyl booths, counter stools, jukebox packed with oldies, and teens on first dates, Snelgrove's evoked a simpler time. Dreyer's still makes a Snelgrove's ice cream line, available in Utah supermarkets, but it's not quite the same.

Around the World in 20 Acres

Salt Lake City

Hey all you globetrotters! Did you know you can see the Eiffel Tower, the Matterhorn, and Copenhagen's Little Mermaid statue without leaving Salt Lake City?

These landmarks and more await visitors to the city's International Peace Gardens, where twenty-eight countries are represented with statues, flower beds, and other memorials.

OK, so the Matterhorn replica is only about 50 feet high—just a wee bit smaller than actual size—and the Eiffel Tower could fit on your coffee table. But where else can you tour the world in the amount of time you'd waste passing through security at the airport?

Tucked away in Jordan Park west of downtown, the peace gardens were established in the aftermath of World War II by the Salt Lake Council of Women—in case you need further proof that women are the less-violent sex. They opened in 1947 on land donated and maintained by the city.

A plaque at the gardens' entrance reads, "America bids the world to be done with the instruments of war and in the spirit of these gardens to cultivate the arts of peace."

Well, we all know how that worked out.

But at least the gardens are fun to look at. Utah immigrants from the respective countries designed each of the twenty-eight sections, guaranteeing a variety of styles. The Chinese garden contains pagodas, the Indian garden has a sculpture of Gandhi, the Italian garden boasts a tiled map of Italy, and Switzerland has its Matterhorn Peak, towering over a little alpine chalet.

The garden has no room for more countries, although there's talk of expanding it across the Jordan River, which runs along its western border.

Paris?! Sorry, no — Salt Lake City.

"We're open to any country that wants to join," says Irene Wiesenberg, the gardens' chairwoman. A native of England, Wiesenberg is especially fond of the British garden with its roses and its bust of former prime minister Margaret Thatcher.

The gardens host a celebration on the third Saturday of August each year with costumes, dancing, and food from many of the countries. You'll find the International Peace Gardens in the west end of Jordan Park, about 1000 South 900 West.

Get Barbie into Surgery, STAT
Salt Lake City

Mary Davidson is not a doctor, but she's healed thousands of patients. She treats anybody, although the vast majority of her patients are girls and women. And no matter how swiftly Mary restores her patients to good health, they never thank her. Except for that Chatty Cathy, they rarely say anything at all.

That's because her patients are dolls. For sixty years now, Mary has been repairing them at Davidson's Antique and Doll Hospital in her family-owned cottage on busy State Street. The ivy-covered "hospital" doesn't look like much from the outside—it's got a hand-painted sign, and its yard is choked with weeds. But its unique services have made many Utah girls very, very happy.

Since 1947 customers have brought their dolls to Mary to fix torn limbs, repair missing hair, or replace lost eyes. Mary is in her nineties now and works from her home instead of the "hospital," but her son Terry runs the shop and still delivers broken dolls each week for her to mend.

The shop is cluttered floor to ceiling with more than one thousand antique and vintage dolls, most of them for sale. Display cases groan with storybook dolls, paper dolls, rag dolls, wooden dolls, wax dolls,

Japanese dolls and, yes, Barbies galore. Many of the dolls date to the 19th century. Others are likenesses of such famous figures as Winston Churchill and Mae West.

Mary Davidson has repaired many of them at one time or another. She once spent hours mending a California man's daughter's teddy bear that had been chewed to pieces by the family dog. Both the man and the girl were so grateful that they sent her thank-you letters.

It's stories like these that keep her going. Whenever she is able to nurse a worn or damaged doll back to health, Mary says, "you know you've done something that has really pleased someone."

Davidson's Doll Hospital is open Wednesday through Saturday from noon to 6:00 p.m. at 2804 South State Street. For more information call (801) 467-6644.

A Taste of Acapulco

Sandy

The Mayan Adventure restaurant is located in the Jordan Commons entertainment complex, but there's nothing common about this family-oriented Mexican eatery. For starters, its cavernous forty thousand-square-foot interior replicates a tropical jungle with abundant foliage, talking toucans and lizards, and terraced tables surrounding a Mayan temple with a 30-foot waterfall.

The themed restaurant, owned by Utah Jazz owner Larry H. Miller, has been a huge hit since it opened in 2000. Maybe it's because kids never get bored waiting for their peanut-butter shakes to arrive. A tropical-flavored petting zoo, supplied by Salt Lake City's Hogle Zoo, provides parrots, iguanas, and other colorful critters. And every so often a "rainstorm" passes through, complete with thunderous sound effects.

The main attraction of the 1,000-seat restaurant, however, is the Acapulco-style cliff diving. Every thirty minutes, a team of divers climbs atop the 30-foot waterfall and plunges into the pool below, adding a few crowd-pleasing flips on the way down. The tiered restaurant is designed so that almost every table has a cliff-diver view. A few unlucky diners may even get splashed.

The Mayan Adventure is open seven days a week in the Jordan Commons complex, 9400 South State Street. Beware: the place is packed most nights, and you may have to wait for a table. For more information call (801) 304-4600.

Milling Around at Gardner Village
West Jordan

While most shopping malls have been around for three or four decades, Gardner Village can trace its history back a little further—to 1853, in fact. That was the year Archibald Gardner, a Mormon convert from Scotland, opened his first flour mill on the site. The mill lasted twenty-four years before Gardner replaced it with a larger one. Today, that 1877 mill has been converted into a restaurant, Archibald's, whose main level has nine booths—each dedicated to one of Archibald's wives.

You see, there's more to Gardner Village than meets the eye. At first glance, the place looks like just another outdoor retail complex—albeit with a fake pioneer village motif and shops spelled "shoppes." But look around for five minutes and you'll realize there's some genuine history here.

Most of the village's twenty-two shops occupy restored historic buildings that were hauled here from around the state. Hamann's Antiques, for example, is in an 1876 miner's cabin. The Rooster House, a crafts store, fills a rare two-story pioneer house, built from hand-hewn

Snowmen greet wintertime visitors to Gardner Village, a slice of early Americana.

logs in 1886 and hauled to the village from Clover, southwest of Tooele. Despite its age the cabin is so sturdy that it shifted less than ⅛-inch during the move.

Gardner Village is the brainchild of Nancy Long, a grandmother who bought the then-abandoned flour mill in 1979 over the objections of her parents, who thought she had lost her mind. Long turned part of the restored mill into a gift shop, then added the restaurant ten years later. That same year, in 1990, she placed newspaper ads stating, "Wanted: Old buildings to be moved," and the village was born.

Although surrounded by parking lots, the complex is laid out so its stores face inward onto a picturesque village green laced with Archibald Gardner's old irrigation canals. Shoppers stroll down brick sidewalks, over wooden bridges, under lampposts, and past country shops with cozy front porches. There's almost no traffic noise. The effect is like going back in time—at least until you hear the piped-in country music.

You'll find no Gap or Body Shop here; all the stores are local, and almost all sell the kind of stuff you might have found in a pioneer shop a century ago: linens, lace, candles, quilts, woodwork, and Christmas ornaments. Let's be honest, though: with shop names like Posh Frippery, Elsa Belle, and Just Us Girls, Gardner Village is not really a place for guys. Sure, it's quaint and all, but fellas, be warned—there's not a sporting goods or electronics store in sight.

Gardner Village is located at 1100 West 7800 South. In the summer months, the village offers pony rides and Barnyard Buddies, a petting zoo.

A Little Off The Top, or Tops Too Little?

West Jordan

"It's always hot at Bikini Cuts," is the telephone greeting at this beach-themed hair salon, where the stylists wear bikinis and the overwhelmingly male clientele try not to stare. Guys wait for their haircuts in electronic massage chairs, where they leaf through such male-oriented reading material as *Maxim,* Victoria's Secret catalogs, and *Guns & Ammo.*

Like Hooters girls, the salon's buxom stylists are showcased in pin-up calendars and photo galleries on its Web site. But don't get the wrong idea.

"We're not strippers," they say. And yes, they actually know how to cut hair.

A few similar-themed salons with female stylists in bathing suits have opened around the country since the first Bikini Cuts debuted in nearby Sandy in 2003, hawking bumper stickers reading, "My Stylist is Hotter Than Yours." But by all accounts, Bikini Cuts was the first.

As you might imagine, this caused a ruckus in socially conservative Utah. Residents complained, and local officials even asked the state's former "porn czar"—unsuccessfully, as it turned out—for help in shutting down the salon or restricting it to neighborhoods zoned for strip clubs. At the same time, Bikini Cuts got an avalanche of media attention, some from as far away as New Zealand.

Community pressure succeeded in thwarting Bikini Cuts' expansion plans. As of spring 2007 only the West Jordan salon remained. But new co-owner Kylee Affleck hopes to open Bikini Cuts salons in other states. "Things have really settled down," she said. "I've only seen one complaint since I've been here."

So, need a, um, haircut? Bikini Cuts is located at 1709 West 7800 South. For an appointment call (801) 562-CUTS.

SHE'S NAILED A WORLD RECORD

When Lee Redmond of Salt Lake City stopped trimming her fingernails in 1979, she had no idea how far they would take her.

Her nails landed her in newspapers, magazines, and the *National Enquirer.* They got her on TV. And in 2006, they took her all the way to London, where she was flown to promote the newest edition of their *Guinness Book of World Records,* featuring her and her record-setting nails, now more than 30 inches long.

"I've done things, met people, and gone places I never would have without them," she says.

Yes, Redmond's nails pose some unique challenges. Getting a manicure takes more than five bottles of nail polish. She can't wear clothes with tight-fitting sleeves. The constant weight makes her fingers ache. She must punch buttons with her knuckles. And people ask her rude questions about how she uses the bathroom. (The answer: Very carefully.)

But the nails have taught her patience. And she's had them for so long now that they feel like part of her identity. Redmond once turned down $10,000 to cut her nails on live Japanese TV.

Maybe the most common question she's asked is whether her fingernails get in her way. No, she says. "They get in everybody else's way but mine. I'm used to them."

Lee Redmond shows off her record-setting fingernails.

NORTHEAST

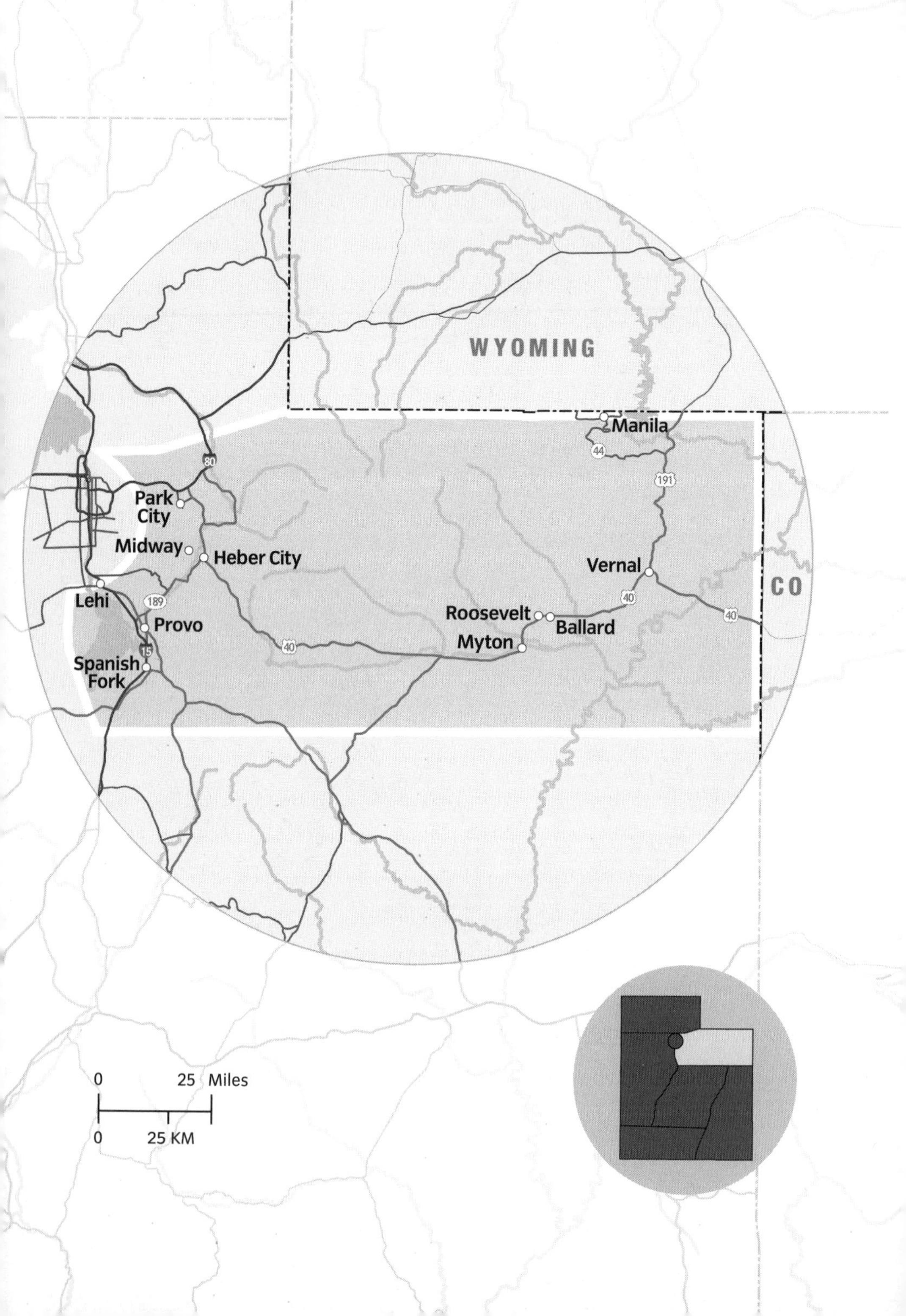

WYOMING

Manila

44

191

Park City

80

Midway

Heber City

Vernal

40

CO

Lehi

189

Roosevelt

Ballard

40

Provo

Myton

Spanish Fork

15

40

0   25 Miles

0   25 KM

NORTHEAST

Does the wide-eyed kid scientist in you still love dinosaurs? Then you'll flip for Utah's northeast corner, which was absolutely teeming with the scaly beasties back in the day. We know this because thousands of their bones are on display at Dinosaur National Monument, home to the world's largest Jurassic dinosaur quarry. Or drive down Vernal's Main Street, where dino statues populate every other block, and you'll see why this part of Utah is nicknamed Dinosaurland.

Even if you yawned through *Jurassic Park,* you'll still find plenty of unique stuff to visit here. Maybe the Sundance Film Festival in Park City, with its offbeat movies and infamous celebrity behavior, is more your scene. Or come in the heat of summer to the cool Uinta Mountains, Utah's highest and one of the only ranges in the world that's oriented east-west.

In fact, consider Northeast Utah a big playground. Where else in the world can you climb into a bobsled and retrace the tracks of Olympians by zipping around a track at 80 mph? Or attend a festival devoted to llamas, or see a famous stuffed liger, or visit the former home of a three-legged dog?

If that's not enough you also can ride on a haunted train, swim inside a crater, reenact Kevin Bacon's flour-mill dance moves in *Footloose,* view a collection of dolls crafted to resemble First Ladies, and get lost in a cornfield grown by the nation's leading corn-maze designer.

So turn the page, and let's do this.

Utah's UFO Ranch
Ballard

Gather 'round the campfire, kids, turn off those flashlights, and listen up. What I'm about to tell you is scary. Real scary. Word is there's this remote ranch in northeastern Utah where bizarre things happen: UFO sightings, cattle mutilations, crop circles, strange voices, and poltergeist activity. That's right, ghosts. And I haven't even gotten to the melting dogs yet. Ooooooooooh.

OK, I'll knock off the spooky-campfire act and tell it to you straight: I'm not sure how much of this stuff is true. There's no hard evidence to support any of these "sightings," and crazy conspiracy theorists are rampant on the Internet. But there's been enough written about this place over the years that *something* weird must be going on.

Known as the Sherman Ranch or Skinwalker Ranch, the property covers some 480 acres of barren rangeland southeast of Ballard. According to media reports and Internet sites, the ranch is owned by the National Institute for Discovery Science (NIDS), a privately funded research organization that studies paranormal activity. The folks at NIDS reportedly bought the place, which includes a farmhouse and several outlying buildings, after its previous owners freaked out about the strange goings-on there.

The most sensationalist reports about the ranch were written by George Knapp, a reporter for the now-defunct *Las Vegas Mercury*, who visited the ranch in 2002. Knapp later combined with NIDS researcher Colm Kelleher on a 2005 book about the ranch. Among their claims, many of them reported by the couple that sold the ranch to NIDS, were anecdotal sightings of RV-size flying objects; a Bigfoot-like creature; doors in the house opening and slamming shut; crop circles appearing in the grass; and glowing orbs that once blasted a dog with lightning, causing it to melt. Poor poochie.

Many of these strange phenomena reportedly happened only once, or reoccurred briefly before stopping altogether, making scientific observation difficult. Observers have floated several possible explanations, including secret military testing, Navajo witchcraft, and the chance that the episodes were caused by mundane beings and events that were misinterpreted by people.

Skeptics, on the other hand, believe the whole thing sounds, well, ridiculous.

I'd encourage you to check it out for yourself, but the ranch is private property, and trespassing is strongly discouraged. One Web site, www.aliendave.com, warns that entering the paranormal hotspot "puts your safety at risk." So think twice before venturing out there. And whatever you do, don't bring your dog.

Heber Creepin'

Heber City

The Heber Valley Railroad has more nicknames than Sean "P. Diddy" Combs. Depending on the duration of the trip and the occasion, Utah's only steam-powered passenger railroad is known alternately as the Provo Canyon Limited, the Soldier Hollow Express, the Old West Casino Train, the Sunset BBQ Special, the Heber Valley Hoedown Train, and the Comedy-Murder Mystery Train.

And that's not counting the train's longest-held and best nickname: the Heber Creeper.

Heber's railroadin' history began in 1899, when the Rio Grande Western Railway began daily service to this mountain valley town. At that time, the line between Heber and Provo was mostly used to ship freight, although the railroad tacked a passenger car onto the end to accommodate demand. Because the train navigated the steep, curving canyon so slowly, passengers dubbed it the "Heber Creeper." One story held that a pair of newlyweds boarded the train in Pravo and gave birth to their first child as the locomotive pulled into the Heber station.

Eclipsed by paved roads and fast cars, the train shut down in 1967. But a group of local businesspeople—OK, train nuts—revived it four years later as a historic attraction. State lawmakers later ponied up more than $1 million to restore the train and keep it running.

Today more than 95,000 passengers ride the trains each year, sitting in vintage coaches pulled by two 1907 Baldwin steam locomotives and three diesel engines. Since the 1980s the trains have been featured in several TV series and more than thirty movies. And during holidays, the Heber Valley Railroad morphs into themed trains such as the Haunted Canyon Limited (Halloween) and the Polar Express (Christmas), complete with elves serving hot chocolate.

Trains depart from a depot at 450 South 600 West. For more information and schedules, visit www.hebervalleyrailroad.org or call (435) 654-5601. For tickets, call (800) 888-TIXX.

Would You Like Fries with That Trainburger?

Heber City

The Dairy Keen's slogan is "Home of the Train," but that's a bit of an understatement. There are at least three trains in this railroad-themed burger joint, which has been serving hungry Heber Valley residents since 1946.

First, you'll notice the colorful kids'-size train on the front lawn—perfect for pint-size engineers. In a front room you'll find a large display case holding a "Harry Potter" train, which, for 25 cents, chugs from King's Cross Station through miniature villages to Hogwarts and back.

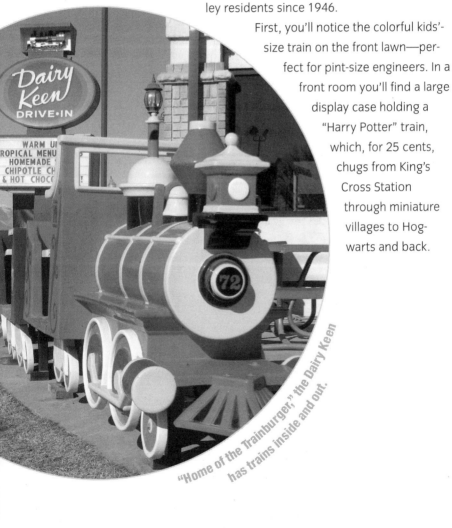

"Home of the Trainburger," the Dairy Keen has trains inside and out.

The Dairy Keen's centerpiece, however, is a little train that circles the restaurant's dining area on an overhead track. Built in the mid-1980s by owner Max Mawhinney, the train celebrates Heber's railroad heritage by passing through scale-model scenes of an Indian village, a stock-yard, the old Heber train depot, and a replica of Heber's historic Main Street (see if you can spot the train robber). Behind the train are murals depicting such local landmarks as Mount Timpanogos and the Jordanelle reservoir.

The train runs in and out of tunnels, followed by a little track-repair truck. During the holiday season the train is given a Christmas makeover, with Santa Claus as the conductor. The constant, six-day-a-week travel takes its toll on the train's eight engines, which are rotated and serviced every two weeks.

The Dairy Keen takes its unusual name from a not-so-unusual source: It used to be a Dairy Queen. The Mawhinney family bought the fast-food eatery in 1968 and planned to turn a quick profit by selling the place and its surrounding land. To save money on signage, they simply replaced the "QU" in "Queen" with a "K." To their surprise, however, the Mawhinneys discovered they loved the fast-food business.

Today the menu's highlights are Trainburgers (featuring a slice of ham and two types of cheese) and more than forty varieties of milk shakes, including Banana Cream Pie and Gummy Bear. Dairy Keen also sells T-shirts with the slogan, "Been Hit By a Trainburger Lately?" Follow your stomach to 199 South Main Street (435-654-KEEN).

UTAH MAY BE A DESERT, BUT IT'S NOT DRY

Because of its dominant Mormon population, whose religion frowns upon alcohol, Utah has a reputation for sobriety. And yes, our liquor laws are a little nutty. But Utah has a long, colorful, and surprising history of liquor-making and consumption, dating back to Mormon pioneers, who were by no means teetotalers.

Brigham Young himself built a distillery and was known to have a nip or two. One of his bodyguards, Orrin Porter Rockwell, owned a brewery. Nineteenth-century Mormons produced their own brand of whiskey, Valley Tan, which was praised by Mark Twain during his 1861 visit to Salt Lake City.

Although the Word of Wisdom—a code of conduct that prohibits Mormons from smoking and drinking alcohol or coffee—originated in 1833, it was not followed strictly by devout Mormons until 1921, during Prohibition, when abstinence was required to be deemed worthy of entering a sacred temple. Ironically, Utah in 1933 became the 36th and deciding state to ratify the 21st Amendment ending Prohibition. Remember that the next time you hoist your glass!

You won't find any hard-liquor manufacturers in Utah. But recent decades have seen an explosion in small and medium-size breweries, some of which poke fun at Utah's image. The Schirf Brewing Company in Park City produces several beers with cheeky names. One, St. Provo Girl Pilsner, comes with a buxom blonde on its label and the slogan, "Baptize your taste buds."

But the brewery's most controversial product is a popular brew called Polygamy Porter. Its label shows a man surrounded by six wives, accompanied by the slogan, "Why Have Just One?"

The Most Curious Man in Utah?

Lehi

John Hutchings made Curious George look blasé. The self-educated Lehi man, who delivered the town's mail from 1918 to 1948, rarely found something that didn't intrigue him. And when he found an item that intrigued him, he began to collect it.

Because Lehi was a small town in those days, Hutchings usually finished delivering the mail by early afternoon, leaving him plenty of time to pursue his many hobbies. He began in the early 1900s with rocks and minerals, then moved on to birds' eggs, American Indian arrowheads, pioneer memorabilia, even a collection of various styles of barbed wire.

John Hutchings with some of his arrowheads.

By 1955 his personal collection had grown so vast that Hutchings donated it to a museum that now bears his name. Its official name is the John Hutchings Museum of Natural History, but that title doesn't even hint at the eclectic nature of the vast collection inside. Although the museum has continued to acquire items since Hutchings's death in 1977, some 85 percent of its collection was gathered in his lifetime.

Among the more noteworthy items are a rifle owned by Butch Cassidy, a Dutch oven reportedly used by George Washington's army at Valley Forge, a set of pistols used by Brigham Young bodyguard Orrin Porter Rockwell, and a seashell-framed mirror owned by former Philippine first lady Imelda Marcos. The museum acquired the mirror as part of a U.S. government liquidation of the Philippine first family's possessions.

Also on display is a toy fire truck collection, a stuffed cobra, a Wild West room with two actual jail cells, flower-like decorations made from human hair, and a woodpecker's tongue that's 5 inches long—four times the length of its beak. The lobby contains a memorial to war veterans, created in 1918, which the museum claims is the first of its kind in the nation.

The John Hutchings Museum of Natural History is open Tuesday through Saturday at 55 North Center Street. For more info, call (801) 768-7180 or visit www.hutchingsmuseum.org.

Footloose and Full of Flour

Lehi

No, millworkers don't spontaneously dance to "Holding Out For a Hero" while loading flour sacks. And to anyone's knowledge, there's never been a high-school prom held inside. But more than two decades after *Footloose* was filmed here, the Lehi Roller Mills keeps churning out flour and pancake mix.

The 1984 movie was filmed entirely in Utah County—filling in for the rural Midwest—including this flour mill, where Kevin Bacon's city-boy Ren character worked when he wasn't getting funny looks for his spiky hair and New Wave wardrobe. To prepare for the role, the then-unknown Bacon even enrolled briefly at Provo High School, where his punky look reportedly didn't go over any better than it did in the movie.

The Lehi Roller Mills almost never made it to the big screen. Fearing that filming at the mill would violate safety regulations, owner Sherman Robinson Jr. initially rebuffed a *Footloose* producer before getting the OK from the state. Although some of Bacon's scenes were shot there, the climactic dance was actually filmed at nearby studios owned by the Osmond family. A scene in which the mill burned down was cut from the film.

The Lehi mill, which opened in 1906, has another claim to fame: Its previous owner, Sherman Robinson Sr., was among the first to extend credit to Pete Harman, who teamed with Harlan Sanders to open the first Kentucky Fried Chicken franchise in Salt Lake City in the 1950s. The mill still makes the cornbread coating mix, with its secret recipe of spices, for more than 200 KFC franchises in the West.

But the mill will always be best known for its *Footloose* cameo. As the movie became a worldwide hit, Robinson needed a full-time employee just to answer the phone calls that poured in from around the country. Fans showed up to get their pictures taken on the porch, where Bacon packaged flour.

The mill celebrated its 100th birthday in 2006 with a free pancake breakfast. Today the only reminder of its *Footloose* history is a framed newspaper clipping hanging in the mill's gift shop, which sells bags of flour and mixes for cookies, muffins, and pancakes. But its place in cinema history lives on everywhere in countless videos, DVDs, and memories.

To visit the mill, take the Lehi exit off Interstate 15. Lehi Roller Mills is at 833 East Main Street, just west of the freeway. Or call (877) 311-3566.

For a while, *Footloose* made this flour mill hip.

THE LAST FLIGHT OF MASASHI GOTO

East of Francis along state Highway 35 is a weathered monument that reads in part, "This monument erected by the Japanese Association of Utah to Masashi Goto 1896–1929 Japanese aviator in his flight over America, Europe and Asia . . . crashed 3,000 feet southeast of this spot."

Surely, you think, there must be more to this story. And there is.

The Japan-born Goto was living in Los Angeles when he and a friend, Takeo Watanabe, decided they would become the first Japanese pilots to make an around-the-world trip. The aviation era was still in its infancy, and anything seemed possible. The men saved for three years and spent $4,500 to build a biplane in Watanabe's garage. When they realized it would be too expensive for both of them to make the journey, it was agreed that Goto, as the oldest, would go solo.

The plan was to hopscotch from L.A. across the country to New York, where Goto and the plane would cross the Atlantic by boat before returning to the skies to cross Europe and Asia. The venture was covered enthusiastically in the Japanese press, and when Goto stopped in Salt Lake City on July 4 to refuel, members of Utah's Japanese-American community greeted him as a hero.

Goto took off again that afternoon and banked his 14-foot-long plane east towards the mountains. Four days later a sheepherder found the wreckage of his little aircraft 8,500 feet above sea level in the Uinta Mountains, Utah's highest range. A search party found his body the next day. In his flight suit they found $300 in cash, a small American flag, and a letter to Watanabe's father in Japan.

Pilots believe Goto flew into a thunderstorm over the mountains and was attempting an emergency landing when he crashed. Both Goto's body and his airplane were shipped back to Southern California, and his dream of aviation glory died more than seventy-five years ago in the Utah mountains. But thanks to this unique monument, he'll never be forgotten.

The A-maze-ing Brett Herbst

Lehi

You might say Brett Herbst is outstanding in his field. The Spanish Fork father of three is Utah's king of the cornfield maze, that annual autumn attraction that sends adults and kids alike wandering happily through rows upon rows of bewildering cornstalks in search of an exit.

Herbst has built more mazes than anyone else in Utah, and his consulting company, The MAiZE, has designed corn mazes in more than forty states and six countries. Now that's agritainment!

A former Idaho ranch boy, Herbst grew up with a passion for agriculture. But he never envisioned his future career until he read an article in a farming magazine about an Englishman who designed America's inaugural corn maze in a Pennsylvania field.

Brett Herbst is outstanding in his field.

Herbst opened his debut maze—the first west of the Mississippi, he says—in 1996. Within three weeks he had 18,000 visitors. By the second year he was getting calls from farmers wanting to build their own mazes. By year three, designing mazes had become a full-time job.

Herbst now spends each spring and summer touring the country, cutting a different maze almost every day. He starts by mapping out a maze on his computer, then marks the field with flags, and mows accordingly when the stalks are only a foot high. Even though people can't see them from the ground, he favors themed designs, which he believes are more fun than rat-maze corridors. In Utah alone, Herbst has designed an Olympics maze, a Bush-Kerry election maze, a *Napoleon Dynamite* maze, and a solar system-themed maze with all the planets. Its title: "Lost in Space."

One of Brett Herbst's a-maze-ing creations.

Despite all his travels Herbst still can be found each fall at his original maze site at the Thanksgiving Point complex in Lehi. Now called Cornbelly's, the field features a different theme each year; after dark, the maze takes on a haunted Halloween flavor, complete with chainsaw-wielding maniacs and other ghoulies who leap from the rows at unsuspecting passersby.

Sure, it's corny. But at admission fees of $10 to $15 a person, Herbst's field is more lucrative than if he harvested the crop. Cornbelly's is open from late September through Halloween. To get there, take exit 284 off I-15 and head northwest past Thanksgiving Point's shops and water tower. For more information visit www.cornbellys.com.

Fire Down Below!
Manila

The Ute Mountain Lookout, where rangers watched for forest fires from living quarters 50 feet above the ground, was the first such tower in the state.

Today, more than seventy years later, it's the last one left.

Completed in 1937 by the Civilian Conservation Corps, the white wooden tower rises above the Ashley National Forest just southwest of Flaming Gorge. Because of its remote location, 30 miles from the nearest town, Forest Service rangers lived in the tower during the summer months and radioed the nearest fire station whenever they spotted a plume of smoke through their binoculars. In other words, Smokey the Bear would have slept here if he could.

In recent years technology doomed the tower as a fire lookout, however. Since the Forest Service began using airplanes, radar, and satellite images to detect forest fires, the Ute Tower has become obsolete.

Listed on the National Register of Historic Places, it's now a monument and an interpretive museum.

Visitors climb the tower's steps to view antiquated fire-locating equipment and learn about the early years of fighting forest fires. Or they just admire the view. From atop its 8,834-foot-high perch, folks on a clear day can see almost 200 miles across the Uinta Mountains and well into Wyoming and Colorado.

The tower is open Friday through Monday from Memorial Day to Labor Day. To get there take Highway 44 to the Sheep Creek Geological Loop, then follow the signs up an unpaved road.

Dive In, the Water's Toasty

Midway

The Homestead has a restaurant, a golf course, a spa, a game room, and . . . yada, yada, yada. But it also has something you won't find at any other resort: a natural rock crater filled with clear blue mineral water bubbling up from the earth at a perfect-for-soaking 90 to 96 degrees.

The Crater, as it's called, began forming about 10,000 years ago when snowmelt seeped into the earth here, heated up, and percolated skyward, depositing minerals that over time formed a beehive-shaped limestone dome.

Shouldn't every resort have a crater?

Resort guests can peek down into the dome from a hole in the top or access the pool through a ground-level tunnel. On the water's surface sit wooden decks from which visitors can bathe, snorkel, or even scuba dive in the 65-foot-deep geothermal pool. The crater hosts a dive shop, and scuba divers come from around the Mountain West, even in winter, to get certified in its warm, effervescent blue waters.

The bottom of the pool is littered with coins, boots, pistols, and other items left decades ago by pioneers and others who used the crater as a watery Dumpster. The Homestead has collected some of these and put them on display inside the resort. So if you lose a watch or something while swimming in the crater, don't be surprised if you return to the Homestead someday and find it in a display case.

The Homestead and its crater are located at 700 North Homestead Drive. For more info call (888) 327-7220.

A Town, a Memories Museum, and a Three-Legged Dog
Myton

On what's left of Main Street in this slumbering town is a historic building whose sign above the front door reads simply, MUSEUM. The door is locked, but Haydon "Bud" Cooper, the museum's curator and town historian, will be happy to come down, show you around, and tell you a story or two.

You might say Bud is fond of the 1910 structure, the last remaining historic building in town. After all, it used to be his grandfather's grocery store. Then it became a pool hall. Today it's filled with historic photos, artifacts, and memorabilia, much of it collected by Bud and Ludy, his late wife and the town's former mayor.

"Bud" Cooper will be happy to show you around his
Myton Memories Museum, located in a former bar.

The building's claim to fame, however, is its legacy, from the 1970s to the late 1980s, as the home of the Three-Legged Dog Saloon. Owner Lou Arnold named the bar for his German shepherd Sidney, who lost his right foreleg after being struck by a car. The bar was popular with the area's oil workers, while Sidney, as its official mascot, was popular with everyone.

When Sidney died in 1983, he'd become so well known that his obituary was printed in *The Salt Lake Tribune*. Lou buried him in a little plot at the bar's southeast corner. The grave is still there, marked by a headstone that reads in part, "Beloved Son of Matilda and Junkyard Dog, Namesake of 3-Legged Saloon, Friend and Companion to its Patrons."

When the saloon closed, the building was reborn as a museum in the early 1990s thanks to a $10,500 donation by longtime Myton resident Babe Odekirk. The Myton Memories Museum, as it's known, displays part of the saloon's wooden bar and mirror along with scores of old photographs of town parades, rodeos, and residents rejoicing at the arrival of electricity. Several photos show Bud as a young man.

The museum also features an old bank-teller window; more than one hundred varieties of barbed wire; a 12½-cent "one bit" coin; a tribute to pro-wrestler-turned actor Phil "The Swedish Angel" Olafsson, who died in Myton; and a government-owned branding iron which, when used, marks the letters "S.U." ("I had it for probably ten years before I realized it was backwards," Bud says.)

"It's a piece of history, I'll tell ya," says Bud of his little museum. "People who come really seem to enjoy it."

For a guided tour call Bud at (435) 722-2280 or the Myton town office at (435) 722-2711.

MOUNTAIN MONOGRAMS

If you visit Provo, you'll notice a giant white "Y" emblazoned on a mountainside above the city. The letter, built in 1906, represents nearby Brigham Young University, which students and alumni call "the Y" for short. Its creators' original plan was to add a B and a U on either side of the block Y, but that never happened.

Some 50 miles to the north, a similar white block "U" sits in the foothills above the University of Utah campus. The "U," which also happens to be the school's nickname, was built in 1907, one year after the big Y at BYU. While the Y is 320 feet high, making it the largest in the nation, the U is lit up during night games and flashes after a Utah victory.

You see, the two schools have a bit of a rivalry going. You might even say they hate each other, especially each November when their football teams clash on the field. Some Utahns call the heated game "the Holy War" because, at least in theory, it pits the Mormons (LDS Church–owned BYU) against the non-Mormons (Utah).

Why? It's shorthand for Brigham Young University.

To students, the giant block letters are symbols of school pride (when BYU's football team won the 1984 national championship, students added a giant "1" to the Y). During the Rivalry Week leading up to the contest, the universities have posted guards by the concrete block letters around the clock to prevent pranksters from the other school from spraying them with paint or smashing the lights that illuminate them at night.

You bet! That's what local folks call the University of Utah.

The Y and the U are among the oldest of the hundreds of hillside letters that commemorate high schools and universities around the West. But their future is in doubt. In 2006 the *Salt Lake Tribune* editorialized against the block U, calling it a "giant environmental scar." And BYU's federal permit to manage the Y, which sits on Forest Service land, expires in 2008.

But don't expect anything to change. Utah's foothills, unmarked by school letters? Y, that would never happen. U must be crazy.

I Wanted Silver and All I Got Was The Shaft

Park City

This resort town's roots lie not in skiing but in mining, which made it one of Old West's rowdiest towns. Its Main Street once was home to twenty-seven saloons; a standing wager, apparently never won, held that nobody could have a drink in each one and remain standing afterwards.

After Park City's last miners stopped pulling silver from the Ontario Mine here in 1982, speculators wondered how to wring more profits from a mine that had already yielded millions of dollars in precious metals. The answer came in 1995, when entrepreneurs reopened the mineshaft as a novel tourist attraction that lowered visitors 1,500 feet into the earth.

Guides outfitted visitors with yellow ponchos and hard hats, then loaded them into an elevator that descended more than a quarter-mile—deeper than the 1,250-foot Empire State Building is tall. It was not a trip for claustrophobics. Visitors then boarded an underground train and traveled east to a spot said to be directly under the wine cellar of Deer Valley Resort's Stag Lodge.

Along the way visitors learned about the mine's colorful history—it was once owned by the father of California newspaper magnate William Randolph Hearst—and how early 20th-century miners lowered horses into the shaft to pull ore cars.

The Silver Mine Adventure, as it was called, attracted almost half a million tourists in four years. But it wasn't enough. The mine did decent business in the summer months but couldn't lure skiers off the nearby slopes in the winter. It closed in 1999.

The mine's operations are still visible alongside the Guardsman Pass road between Park City and Deer Valley. But for now, it's strictly an above-ground curiosity.

Sledding and Shredding

Park City

Ever dream of competing in the Winter Olympics? Or do you just like to go really, really fast? Either way, you'll get a thrill from the Utah Olympic Park, where visitors can climb into a bobsled and hurtle around an icy track at speeds of up to 80 mph.

The park hosted bobsled, luge, skeleton, and ski-jumping events during the 2002 Winter Olympics and serves as a year-round training center for world-class athletes. But regular folks can use it, too. The admission fee includes a self-guided tour of the competition venues and access to a museum devoted to Utah's Olympic history.

A brave rider readies for a summer bobsled run.

But the real thrill is the "Comet" bobsled, which navigates the entire actual Olympic track and makes most roller coasters feel like a donkey ride. In the winter, guests accompany an experienced driver around the track while experiencing five Gs of force—the equivalent of a forty-story drop in less than a minute.

Riders must be at least sixteen years old, don helmets, and sign a liability waiver before climbing into the sled. "This is a very aggressive ride," warns the park's Web site, which discourages passengers who are pregnant, have had recent surgery, or who suffer from neck or back problems. Rides in the winter run $200 per person. Visitors can save money by trying the ride in the summer, when the sleds race around a concrete track on wheels instead of runners. The summer sleds travel about 10 mph slower than their winter counterparts but cost $65.

Ready to go 80 mph, fellas?

In summer the park also offers introductory lessons for freestyle ski jumpers who practice aerial flips into a large splash pool. The lessons are available to skiers and snowboarders of all ages. Also at the park is the interactive Alf Engen Ski Museum, at which visitors can grip ski poles and take a virtual-reality run down the Olympic downhill course at Snowbasin.

The park is located off Highway 224 between Interstate 80 and downtown Park City. Admission is $8 for adults; $6 for kids under eighteen. For more info, call (435) 658-4200 or visit www.utaholympic park.com.

THE SKIERS' SUBWAY

The world's first underground ski lift opened in 1965 in an old silver mine shaft at the now-defunct Treasure Mountain Resort in Park City. Skiers climbed into modified miners' trolleys and were pulled 2½ miles through the pitch-black Spiro Tunnel—dug to drain water from the mine—to an old mine elevator that lifted them 1,750 feet to the surface.

Two-and-a-half minutes after entering the elevators, skiers emerged, blinking in the sun, near the Thaynes chair lift, from which they could access the entire mountain. Operated by miners, the lift offered a memorable experience. But the "skier's subway," as it was called, lasted only four years. Because it was cold, clammy, and dark, some skiers thought it was creepy.

Grit, Glitz, and Paris Hilton, Too

Park City

Held the third week of January each year, the Sundance Film Festival is the largest event in the country devoted to independent film. But that's not what makes it weird. What began as a small, cultish event for edgy filmmakers and hardcore film buffs has mushroomed into a frenzied ten-day happening full of glitzy premieres, corporate parties, and a crush of rubberneckers hoping for a glimpse of someone famous.

With so much craziness packed into a small ski town, there's bound to be some misbehavin'. There was the year that Park City police towed film critic Roger Ebert's illegally parked car—twice. Or the year that Miramax chief Harvey Weinstein went ballistic in a Park City restaurant after losing the rights to *Shine*. Or the year the premiere of a movie called *American Pimp* attracted a handful of real pimps and their entourages, causing a near-riot when there weren't enough seats.

The festival draws thousands of film-industry types from Los Angeles and New York, most of them dressed in stylish winter gear and barking into cell phones. Locals have a nickname for them: PIBs, or People in Black. It's not a compliment. Oh, and Robert Redford usually shows up, too.

In recent years, the festival has also attracted celebrities such as Paris Hilton who come for the parties, the paparazzi, and the free swag. As a result, parties are notoriously hard to get into. One bouncer, surveying the desperate throng outside his door, famously shouted, "Nobody is getting in unless you're famous, and I don't recognize any of you!"

It's also drawn parasitic grass-roots film festivals that set up camp in town the same week, including Tromadance (devoted to B-movies), Vandance (a guy showing his movie in his van, parked on Main Street), and Lapdance (I'm not sure what this was, but there were strippers involved).

In fairness, Sundance has also launched the careers of such auteurs as Steven Soderbergh and Quentin Tarantino, along with such influential films as *Clerks, The Blair Witch Project,* and *Napoleon Dynamite.* You never know when you're going to see an unknown filmmaker be crowned the next Scorsese overnight.

If you love film—and don't mind a steady diet of sex, violence, hipster irony, and low production values—it's still possible to show up without tickets and wrangle your way into a screening or two. Screenings also are held in Salt Lake City and in Ogden, but, come on—who cares? For celebrity-spotting, parking hassles, and a frenetic winter-carnival atmosphere, the only place to be during Sundance is Park City.

For more info about the festival visit www.sundance.org.

Shasta the Liger
Provo

As any fan of *Napoleon Dynamite* knows, a liger is a cross between a lion and a tiger. And, yes, they actually exist. Ligers, although rare, are created when a male lion is bred in captivity with a female tiger.

One of the first and only ligers in the country was born May 14, 1948, at the Hogle Zoo in Salt Lake City after keepers allegedly housed a female Bengal tiger briefly in the zoo's lion cage and nature took its course.

Call me a liger, please: The late Shasta.

"SHASTA" THE LIGER

Called Shasta because "she hasta" have this and "she hasta" have that, the bossy liger—she was a ligress, to be more precise—was one of the zoo's most beloved and famous residents before she died in 1972 at the ripe age of twenty-four.

But Shasta lives on. After her death she was stuffed and displayed in the zoo's feline house. Eventually, however, the zoo director felt that because such a creature would never exist in the wild, Shasta should find another home. In 1999 she was moved to the Monte L. Bean Life Sciences Museum on the campus of Brigham Young University, where anyone can visit her today.

BYU occasionally loans Shasta back to Hogle Zoo for special appearances, such as the zoo's 75th birthday in 2006. By the way, BYU is where the makers of *Napoleon Dynamite* went to film school. Coincidence? I think not.

You'll find the Monte L. Bean Life Sciences Museum at 645 East 1430 North. For more info call (801) 422-5051 or visit www.mlbean.byu.edu.

Time for Some Pie

Provo

Kristin Murdock knows a thing or two about entrepreneurism. Or should that be entre-*manure*-ism?

From her home in Provo, the mother of five sells clocks, mirrors, plaques, and other items made from, um, cow pies. Yes, that's right. Murdock collects dried cow dung from the Utah desert, shellacs it, drills holes in it, and then stuffs it with small mirrors or battery-powered clocks. Don't worry, they're odorless.

You need a sense of humor to do something like this, and Murdock has one. Each pie comes with a little pun, such as "Been There, Dung That," or "A Chip Off the Old Block." She adorns her cow-pie picture frames with the slogan, "A Picture is Worth a Thousand Turds." Her Employee-of-the-Month plaques read, "You Are Outstanding in Your Field." Her cow-pie mirrors read, "You Look Like Crap."

It all started in 1998 when Murdock was hiking in southern Utah and stumbled across a batch of dried cow droppings. She picked one up and thought, "I could make something out of this." Soon she was giving her cow-pie creations to friends and relatives as gag gifts.

This is where Donny Osmond comes in. Through a friend of the family, the singer and former teen idol heard about Murdock's clocks and requested one. A few weeks later Murdock tuned in to *Donny & Marie*, the TV talk show, to hear Donny and his kid sister laughing about her cow-pie clocks.

"She can't make 'em fast enough," Osmond chuckled, holding one up for the cameras as the studio audience cheered. "The cows can't make 'em fast enough."

That's entre-manure-ism: Kristin Murdock and one of her cow-pie clocks.

A *Donny & Marie* staffer contacted Murdock the next day to say the show was getting calls from viewers who wanted to buy cow-pie clocks. And Murdock's business was born.

She now sells her creations for up to $49.95 through her Web site, www.cowpieclocks.com. Or call (801) 225-1152. And be prepared for some bad puns—Murdock has a pastureful of them.

Is The Honeymoon Over for Bridal Veil Falls?
Provo

There are twenty-three waterfalls in the United States named Bridal Veil Falls. But only one had a 1,700-foot rickety tram that shuttled tourists from the bottom to the top and was billed as the world's steepest aerial tramway. When they weren't hiding their eyes, tram riders enjoyed the bird's-eye views of the 607-foot, two-tiered falls, which cascade down a cliff to the Provo Canyon floor below.

Today the six-passenger tram is gone, wiped out by a massive avalanche in 1996. The 1,000-foot-wide snowslide cascaded down the cliff at 200 mph, uprooting hundreds of trees, damming the Provo River, and burying the highway under 50 feet of powder. It also buried the tram's snack bar and souvenir shop under a pile of rubble.

Designed in Switzerland and installed in 1961, the seasonal tram became one of Utah's most popular attractions. On peak days in the summer, tourists waited in line more than two hours to ride to the top of the falls, where a cliff's edge restaurant hosted dinners and dances. Once a tram operator accidentally stranded a young couple overnight in a gondola suspended hundreds of feet above the ground. Rescuers found them, cold but unhurt, the next day.

The Grow family, which has owned the property since 1974, believes the tram can be rebuilt. Spared by the avalanche but ransacked by vandals, the old restaurant still stands atop the falls. But restoring the entire resort would cost at least $2.5 million—money the family doesn't have.

So Wyatt Grow and his relatives are seeking investors. They have commissioned an engineering study and lobbied elected officials for help. A proposed new tram's gondolas would seat ten people and reach the top of the falls in less than five minutes.

In the meantime, lovebirds continue to exchange wedding vows beside the falls. And during the winter months the frozen falls attract ice climbers from around North America. One especially popular route up the ice is called Stairway to Heaven. The Grows hope someday visitors will have the option of skipping the stairs and taking a Tramway to Heaven instead.

Bridal Veil Falls are located near the south end of Provo Canyon, a five-minute drive east of Provo on Highway 189.

All Dolled Up but Nowhere To Go

Provo

For almost twenty-five years, the McCurdy Historical Doll Museum enchanted doll lovers of all ages with its vast collection, which included likenesses of such famous figures as Cleopatra, Joan of Arc, Martha Washington, Queen Victoria, and Shirley Temple. At its peak the museum housed some 4,000 dolls and was a popular stop for tour buses.

"It's a magnificent collection," says Shirley Paxman, who ran the attraction with her husband Monroe. "People came from all over the United States just to see that museum."

But the Paxmans, who are in their eighties, finally retired in 2002 and closed the museum, which they operated from a historic carriage house on their property at 246 North 100 East. The couple wants to display the collection intact, preferably near Provo, and assumed that

Monroe and Shirley Paxman with some of their many dolls.

another museum would offer the dolls a permanent home. But finding just the right adoptive parents, so to speak, has proved harder than anyone expected.

The collection started when Shirley Paxman began saving dolls that belonged to her eight sisters and five daughters. Her nascent hobby got a huge boost when she was given 800 dolls belonging to Laura McCurdy Clark, a Utah widow who had been collecting them since the early 1900s. Other Utahns donated their dolls, too, and the collection mushroomed.

Among the thousands of dolls on display were heroines from Charles Dickens novels, Beatrix Potter figures, Dr. Seuss characters, dolls representing women of the Bible, dolls displaying clothing styles from different eras and, yes, several original busty Barbies—with beau Ken, of course. Some of the dolls date back more than 200 years.

The Paxmans don't want to see their beloved dolls languish in storage much longer. As of spring 2007 they were still actively looking for a new museum site. By the time you read this, they may have succeeded; check with the Utah Valley Convention & Visitors Bureau at (801) 370-8393.

Also near Provo:

The Sundance resort, Robert Redford's rustic getaway in a scenic canyon above the valley. Besides its ski slopes, restaurant, cabins, and movie-screening room, Sundance is notable for its Owl Bar, a restored 1890s saloon relocated here from Thermopolis, Wyoming. Legend has it the bar was frequented back in the day by Butch Cassidy's Hole-in-the-Wall Gang, which, of course, included a certain young outlaw nicknamed the Sundance Kid. Redford himself keeps a cabin here and pops in from time to time. For more info visit www.sundanceresort.com.

Marion the Contrarian

Roosevelt

Marion's Variety is named for its founder, Marion Mortensen, a hard-working Danish immigrant who, contrary to the customs of her day, bore children without ever marrying. "I don't have time for a man," she'd say. "I clean up after people [at the store] all day long. I don't want to go home and clean up after another one."

After opening her general store in 1933, Marion moved it ten years later to its current location in a former saloon. Management of the historic landmark and its lunch counter have passed down through Marion's son Eldon to her grandson, Chad Mortensen, who now runs the place with help from his sister, Marisa, and several other relatives.

Chad Mortensen serves a mean milk shake at this one-of-a-kind store and lunch counter named for his grandmother.

"I started working here when I was able to look over the counter," says Chad, an amiable fellow now entering middle age. "Back then we were open til 11 o'clock at night, so if you wanted to see your parents, you had to come down to the store."

Besides its long history—Robert Redford once ate here while shooting *Jeremiah Johnson*—Marion's is notable for two things. The first is its old-fashioned lunch counter, one of several remaining in Utah with chrome-and-vinyl stools and a working soda fountain. Judging by the ham-and-egg and Spam sandwiches, the menu hasn't changed much over the years. The prices haven't, either: You can still get a cheeseburger, chips, and a large milk shake for less than $5.

The second thing is the sheer variety of the knickknacks that fill every inch of the cramped store from the floor to the ceiling. Among the thousands of items for sale: bottles of hot sauce, NASCAR action figures, sheet music, poker chips, tea kettles, wind chimes, clocks, belt buckles, vintage Coca-Cola trays, and bubble-gum ice cream.

"We try to have something for everyone," says Chad, following the example of his grandmother, who died in the early 1990s. "She sold a little bit of everything. If you didn't see it, you just asked."

Marion's Variety is located at 29 North 200 East in the heart of town (435-722-2143).

UTAH'S FURRIEST MOVIE STARS

Grizzly bears became extinct in Utah in the 1920s, but don't tell that to Doug and Lynne Seus. You may not have heard of the Heber couple, but you almost certainly know their pet Bart the Bear, arguably Hollywood's most famous animal since Lassie.

Remember the fierce grizzly who wrestled Brad Pitt in *Legends of the Fall*? That was Bart. The furry critter Anthony Hopkins and Alec Baldwin encountered in *The Edge*? Bart again. The big fella—he stood over 9 feet tall and weighed 1,500 pounds—appeared in more than three dozen feature films, TV shows, and documentaries.

Born in a zoo, Bart came to the Seuses in 1977 as a 5-pound Kodiak cub. As animal trainers, the couple had worked mostly with wolves, cats, dogs, and horses; grizzly bears were something else entirely. But with the Seuses' patience and guidance—and a lot of treats—Bart became a natural in front of the camera. He was even known to wrap his enormous jaws playfully around Doug's head.

"Of all the movie stars I've ever worked with, Bart the Bear is as talented . . . as the best of them," says *Legends of the Fall* director Ed Zwick. "He takes no time at all in makeup, never wants to stay in his trailer, and does all his own stunts."

Bart's movie career took him to Alaska, Europe, and even the 1998 Oscars, where he ambled on stage to give an envelope to presenter Mike Myers, who then quipped, "I just soiled myself."

Bart died of old age in 2000, but his ursine onscreen legacy lives on in the Seuses' newer bears: Tank, Little Bart, and his sister Honey Bump, all of whom appeared opposite Eddie Murphy in *Dr. Dolittle 2*. All the bears also are ambassadors for Vital Ground, the Seuses' non-profit that seeks to preserve North America's vanishing grizzly habitat.

But they'll probably always be best known for their roles in movies, in which they roar, fetch, roll over, scratch their tummies, and wave "bye-bye" on cue.

Hare Krishna, Hare Llama

Spanish Fork

Sure, most summer festivals have food, music, and entertainment. But how many can say they have llamas—and lots of 'em?

Since 1995 the Llama Fest has drawn thousands of revelers each July for a llama pack race, a llama obstacle-course race, a petting zoo, and a "Beautiful Baby Llama" contest. Also offered are Andean crafts, vegetarian food, and demonstrations of shearing, wool-spinning, and hoof-cutting techniques. Each year up to 100 llamas attend, along with their owners, from all over Utah.

The festival is sponsored by Utah Valley Llamas, an offshoot of Utah's only Hare Krishna temple—the first such temple in the nation built from scratch—which opened here in 2001. The event takes place each July on the grassy grounds of the ornate, multi-domed temple,

This Hare Krishna temple hosts a Llama Fest each July.

which also is home to KHQN, the country's only full-time Hare Krishna radio station.

The festival and the temple are the brainchild of Christopher and Christine Warden, Krishna converts who moved to Spanish Fork in 1982 to run the radio station, which offers Indian sari music, swami lectures, and shows on vegetarianism. After years of fund-raising, the couple purchased land and built the temple almost entirely with the help of volunteers—including, remarkably, neighboring members of the Mormon Church, who donated $25,000.

South American llamas have nothing in common with the Hare Krishna culture or religion, whose roots are Indian. But in Spanish Fork the two groups have co-existed harmoniously. In the early years, proceeds from the Llama Fest went towards construction of the temple. Today, several dozen llamas roam the temple grounds along with parrots, peacocks, and pot-bellied pigs.

The Sri Sri Radha Krishna Temple is open to visitors daily at 8628 South Main Street, just south of town. The temple offers tours, hot vegetarian meals, a gift shop and, of course, llamas. For more information on the temple or Llama Fest, call (801) 798-3559 or visit www.utah krishnas.com.

O Jackie, You're Such a Doll!

Vernal

This ranching town in the Uintah basin has nothing in common with Washington, D.C., but that didn't stop some enterprising Vernal women from creating a collection of dolls modeled after First Ladies of the United States. The dolls, each with a facial likeness of a different First Lady, fill three display cases at the Uintah County Library.

A Jackie Kennedy doll, part of a First Ladies doll exhibition at the Vernal Library.

The exhibit is believed to be the only one of its kind in the country, meaning that nowhere else will you see a foot-high Jackie Kennedy standing proudly next to a foot-high Mamie Eisenhower, each wearing a little formal evening gown.

Inspired by an exhibit of First Ladies' gowns in a Smithsonian Institution museum in Washington, a local committee of women launched the project to celebrate America's bicentennial in 1976. They hired Phyllis Juhlin Park, a doll sculptor from a suburb of Salt Lake City, to fashion each doll's head from porcelain (the dolls' bodies are cloth stuffed with sawdust). Meanwhile, Uintah County's best seamstresses sewed miniature replicas of actual dresses worn by the First Ladies.

A Nancy Reagan doll, another one of the First Ladies dolls at the Vernal Library.

While the Martha Washington doll sits, knitting, in a rocking chair, all the other First Ladies are standing. Abigail Adams holds a Bible; Angelica Van Buren looks resplendent in blue velvet; Mary Todd Lincoln holds an Oriental fan; Grace Coolidge carries what looks like an enormous pink feather duster; and Nancy Reagan wears a sleeveless, off-the-shoulder beaded pink gown.

Some presidents are represented by more than one doll. The term "First Lady" refers not just to a president's wife but to the official White House hostess; wives who became too ill to fulfill their hosting duties were succeeded as First Ladies by sisters, daughters, and even daughters-in-law.

Unfortunately, the collection ends with Nancy Reagan. Park, the doll sculptor, retired before she could complete likenesses of Barbara Bush, Hillary Clinton, and Laura Bush. Project leaders still hope to complete the collection; the challenge has been locating a dollmaker with Park's skills and talent.

"We've tried and tried," says local historian Doris Burton, who wrote a brochure about the project. "But we've been unable to find somebody to do it."

Nominees are welcome. The First Ladies of the White House Doll Exhibit is located inside the Uintah County Library, 155 East Main Street. For hours or more info call (435) 789-0091.

"Remember the Maine," and Pass the Climbing Rope

Vernal

It's odd enough that a little park in rural Utah is called "Remember the Maine Park" in honor of the U.S. battleship that exploded and sank in Havana, Cuba, in 1893, precipitating the Spanish-American War. The park is located in a canyon on the outskirts of Vernal—hundreds of miles from any ocean harbor, let alone Maine or Havana.

But it's really strange that across the road from the park, high up a 350-foot cliff face, someone has painted a large American flag onto the rock accompanied by the words, "Remember the Maine," which became a rallying cry for American troops during the war. The flag is almost 100 feet off the ground, so unless it was painted by a giant, someone must have shimmied up there with cans of red, white, and blue paint—an impressive feat.

How'd they paint that thing? This memorial, complete with American flag, is almost 100 feet up a cliff face.

Somebody did. The original slogan, "Remember the Maine," was done in 1898 at the request of a state lawmaker who paid a sailor, L.O. Voight, $50 to do the job. A group of men lowered Voight on a swing over the edge of the cliff.

During World War II, a construction worker named Earl Goodrich noticed the painted letters were fading. So he scaled the cliff on a custom-built scaffold, repainted them, and added "Pearl Harbor" plus a 10-foot-long American flag with forty-eight stars—one for each state at the time. Earl must have been nervous up there, because he painted the blue-and-white star field in the wrong corner. Soon afterwards the flag was repainted to correct his mistake.

Several Boy Scouts repainted the patriotic mural again in 1997, but they didn't try to update the flag by adding stars for Alaska and Hawaii. Said their scout leader, "We want to preserve history."

The park is located in Dry Fork Canyon, 7 miles northwest of town (the actual coordinates are 3500 West 4250 North).

Also near Vernal:

The Flaming Gorge–Uintas Scenic Byway, also called the "Drive Through the Ages." Known officially as Highway 191, it climbs from Vernal to the Flaming Gorge reservoir, passing through millions of years of geologic history until it reaches the 1-billion-year-old exposed core of the Uinta Mountains. Signs along the route trace the changing geologic layers.

DINOS, DINOS EVERYWHERE

Jurassic Park made a dinosaur lover of almost every kid in America, but nowhere in the country are folks quite as dino-crazy as Northeast Utah.

For starters, the region is home to several world-class dinosaur digs. The Cleveland-Lloyd Dinosaur Quarry near Price has produced more than 12,000 dino bones; its skeletons are on display in sixty-five museums around the globe.

Then there's Dinosaur National Monument east of Vernal, home to the largest and most prolific quarry of Jurassic–era dinosaur fossils ever discovered. A sandstone wall inside the visitor center (which was closed as of summer 2007 for structural repairs) contains more than 2,000 exposed dinosaur bones.

Ground zero for dinosaur lovers in Utah may be Vernal, which boasts not one but two giant dinosaur statues at either end of town. Along Main Street to the west is a fierce-looking green T-Rex, while at the eastern end stands a pink, cartoonish—and, judging by the eyelashes, female—brontosaurus. Dinosaur logos are used to advertise dozens of local businesses.

Vernal also has one of the state's finest dinosaur museums: the Utah Field House of Natural History, which contains interactive displays on fossil digs, a walk-through prehistoric forest, and an outdoor sculpture garden with life-size T-Rexes, allosauruses (the Utah state dinosaur), and other scaly beasts.

This pink and presumably female dinosaur welcomes visitors to Vernal.

Stop by the museum for your very own Dinosaur Hunting License—issued, tongue firmly in cheek, by the "U.S. Reptile Control Commission" and signed by "Al O'Saurus, Deputy Lizard Warden." Each license bears the same permit number: I81-UO22, which translates roughly as (say it aloud), "I ate one, you ought to, too."

WEST DESERT

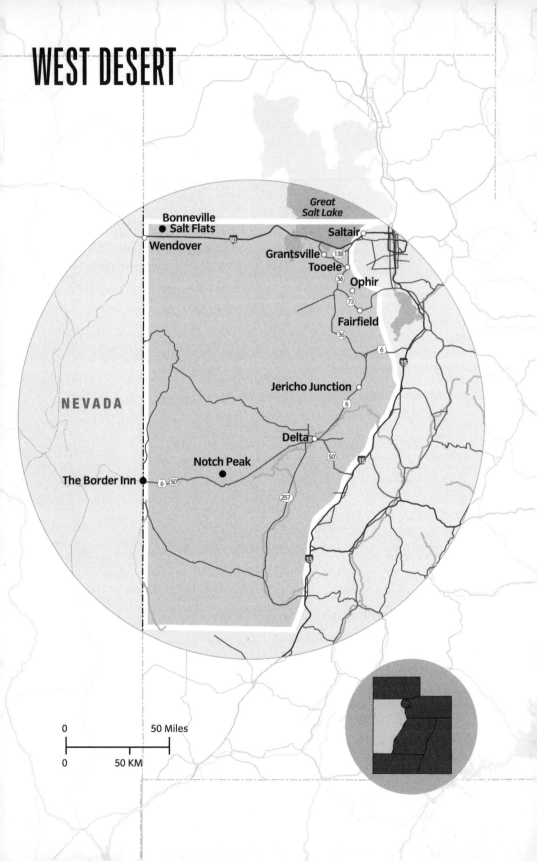

Great
Salt Lake

Bonneville
● Salt Flats
Wendover ○
80

Saltair ○
Grantsville ○
138
Tooele ○
36
Ophir ●
73
Fairfield
36
6
15

NEVADA

Jericho Junction ○
6

Delta ○
50
15
Notch Peak ●
The Border Inn ●
6 50
257

15

0   50 Miles
├─────────┤
0   50 KM
├─────────┤

WEST DESERT

Highway 50, which traverses Utah's west desert before continuing across Nevada, has been called the "loneliest highway in America," and it's not hard to see why. If it wasn't an interstate, the same could be said for the stretch of Interstate 80 from the Salt Lake Valley west to the Nevada line. These roads pass through vast, desolate basins filled with more jackrabbits than people.

But that doesn't mean there's nothing to see out here—beginning with the otherworldly landscape itself. Take the Bonneville Salt Flats, setting for countless car commercials, whose endless white flatness contains enough salt to flavor a pitcher of margaritas for every drinker in the world.

Or an off-roaders' playground called "Little Sahara" for its acres of sandy dunes. Or a mountain that rumbles like your uncle Fred after a chili dinner. Or a lava-rock formation that eerily resembles the profile of Mormon Church founder Joseph Smith. Folks who live out here tend to be an individualistic breed, which is why you'll find the remains of a lost Polynesian colony; a 60-foot-deep hot spring filled with tropical fish; an enormous, "tree"-like sculpture in the middle of nowhere; a star-crossed, Taj Mahal–like beach resort-turned-concert hall; and a historic airbase that was home to the Enola Gay and its crew.

Not to mention a Juke Box Cave. And Paul Bunyan's Woodpile. And . . . well, you'll see.

Will Smith Punched an Alien Here

Bonneville Salt Flats

At first glance, they look like an endless plain covered with snow. Walk out on the flats and the white crust crunches beneath your feet. Sure, you may already think you know this place through such movies as *Independence Day, The World's Fastest Indian,* and the *Pirates of the Caribbean* sequel. But nothing can quite prepare you for the vast, blinding whiteness—a place so flat and broad that you can see the curvature of the earth.

Did you know the salt in places is 6 feet deep? Or that it prevents the growth of all plant life—even those pesky weeds? Or that each winter, a shallow layer of water floods the flats? During the spring and summer, the water evaporates and the wind smooths the surface for miles, making it perfect for what the Bonneville Salt Flats are best known for: high-speed auto racing.

Don't forget to wash your feet!

The salt flats' potential for speed records was discovered in 1896 by an adventurer scouting a potential bicycle-race course from New York to San Francisco. By the 1940s the flats were the world's foremost location for speed merchants pushing souped-up vehicles to go ever faster. By the 1960s jet-powered vehicles driven by such famous thrill-seekers as Craig Breedlove were topping 600 mph.

Each summer the Utah state highway folks re-create the Bonneville Speedway by marking the flats with broad black lines. The speedway typically includes a 10-mile straightaway and a nearby oval for distance runs. Racers from around the world still descend upon the flats every August for Speed Week, a convention of sorts for the speed-junkie crowd.

Visitors to the speedway during other times of the year won't find a track—just a dead-end paved road, a battered sign, and plenty of looping tire marks on the flats left by amateur joy-riders who can't resist taking their cars for spins.

You can access the salt flats from exit 4 off I-80, 4 miles east of the Nevada border. Further east along the interstate is a rest area that also offers a good view of a landscape that's unlike any other in the world.

A Tree Grows on Bonneville
Bonneville Salt Flats

It rises up from the flat white desert landscape like a mirage: an 87-foot-high artistic marvel—sculpture seems too tame a word—called *Metaphor: The Tree of Utah.* The bizarre tree-like structure was created by a Swedish sculptor named Karl Momen after he supposedly saw a vision of a tree in the desert while driving through Utah to California.

Momen funded the project himself and donated it to the state of Utah after it was dedicated in 1986. (Considering that nobody lives for miles around, who would object?) Constructed from 225 tons of cement, almost 2,000 ceramic tiles, and native Utah rocks and minerals, the sculpture stands along I-80 at the edge of the famous Bonneville Salt Flats.

Although stopping along the interstate is discouraged—Momen didn't pay for an exit ramp—many motorists can't resist pulling off onto the shoulder for a closer look. The colorful spheres on the Tree's "branches" resemble billiard balls, or maybe planets in some strange parallel universe.

Inscribed on the Tree's trunk are lyrics from Schiller's "Ode to Joy," from the choral climax of Beethoven's Ninth Symphony. Near the base are several rounded shells reminiscent of fallen leaves. Two-ton leaves, that is.

You'll find the sculpture 26 miles east of Wendover, just to the north of the interstate.

They sure grow strange trees on the salt flats.

Goose on the Loose

Delta

Forget Punxsutawney Phil. Folks here have their own wild animals telling them each winter that spring is on the way.

Like those famous swallows returning to Capistrano, huge flocks of snow geese descend each February on the tiny Gunnison Bend Reservoir on the Sevier River outside of town. The man-made lake is an annual rest stop on the birds' annual 3,000-mile migration from Southern California to their breeding grounds in the Arctic.

As many as 30,000 geese gather at the reservoir every late winter to sip the water and feed on leftover grain or green shoots from nearby alfalfa fields. They start arriving around Valentine's Day, honking constantly, and are gone by mid-March.

The return of the geese is so clockwork-reliable that in the 1990s Delta townsfolk started a two-day festival to celebrate their arrival. The dates of the Snow Goose Festival are set months in advance, but they've never had to be changed for lack of geese. Hey, if someone is throwing a party in your honor, you wanna be there.

Festival events, now spread over two weekends, include a craft fair, quilt show, wildlife photography workshops, and a 10k run called the Wild Goose Chase. And, of course, lots and lots of bird-watching. State wildlife officers set up telescopes to give better views to the 1,500 goose-spotters who attend.

For festival dates and more information call (435) 864-4316.

THE MORMON METEOR

David Abbott Jenkins was a wholesome Mormon country boy who didn't swear, smoke, or drink liquor. But boy, did he love to go fast.

In the early 1900s "Ab," as he was known, raced goat-pulled wagons down the streets of Salt Lake City. But his career as a speed king didn't take off until 1926, when he bet he could outrace a commuter train from New York to San Francisco. Jenkins and a pal drove a Studebaker coast to coast in eighty-six hours—beating the train by some fourteen hours.

By the 1930s, the stocky, white-haired Jenkins was breaking speed records on the Bonneville Salt Flats. His feats drew the attention of world-renowned speedsters like Sir Malcolm Campbell and automakers such as Augie Duesenberg, who custom-built Ab a supercharged car with almost 400 horsepower.

Jenkins, who somehow also found time to serve as Salt Lake City's mayor, dubbed the racecar the Mormon Meteor. It was soon refitted with an aircraft engine and named Mormon Meteor II. By 1940, Ab was assaulting record books in a new car, the 750-hp Mormon Meteor III. Using a circular track on the flats, he once drove 3,000 miles at an average speed of 165 mph. The Meteor's last record run came in 1950, when Jenkins brought the car out of retirement and hit 199 mph.

Ab set his final speed record in a stock car at the age of seventy-three. He died of a heart attack two months later, fittingly, while riding in a car (luckily for everyone involved, he was a passenger). Some of his speed records stood for almost half a century.

The Mormon Meteor III, which Ab sold to the state of Utah for $1, is now valued at $5 million, making it one of the most expensive cars in the world. Ab's son Marvin Jenkins later reclaimed and restored the Mormon Meteor III, which lives on today at classic car shows around the country.

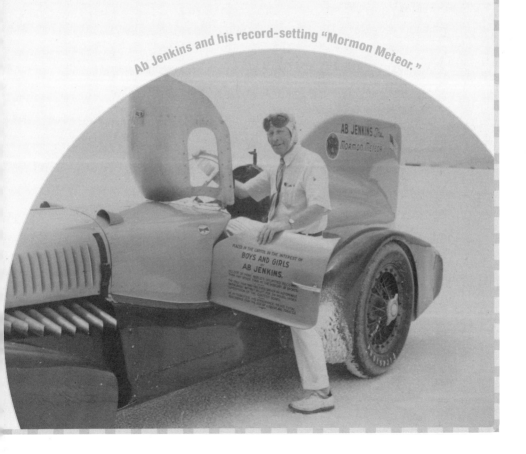

Ab Jenkins and his record-setting "Mormon Meteor."

What a Stone Face
Delta

Joseph Smith, founder and first president of the Mormon Church, was murdered by an angry Illinois mob in 1844. So imagine Mormon pioneers' surprise when they arrived in Utah three years later, fanned out across the desert and discovered a rock outcropping that was the spitting image of their slain prophet.

Called the Great Stone Face, the 35-foot-high rock formation perches atop a lava flow ridge in the remote desert southwest of Delta. From the west, it does resemble Smith's profile—at least the one captured in portraits during his lifetime—and appears to be smiling. The rock has a dual personality, however: When viewed from the east, it's known as the "Devil's Chimney."

From close-up, the rock just looks like a rock, albeit with some big chunks missing, like a stone face with leprosy. Some locals believe Spanish explorers sculpted the face as a directional indicator to help them find their buried gold.

For centuries native Indians no doubt saw their own images in the outcropping, which may explain why its official name is the Great Stone Face and not Joseph's Rock, or something like that.

To find the Great Stone Face, go west from Delta on Highway 50, then head south on Highway 257. In 4 miles, you'll see a sign marking the turnoff to the right. Travel 7 miles on an improved gravel road around the north edge of the lava flow until you see the face. If you want a closer look, a trail leads up the ridge to its base.

Mormon Church founder Joseph Smith.

A coincidence, or Joseph Smith's profile?

THE DESERET ALPHABET

If you browse through the rare-book rooms of Utah's used bookstores, you'll come across an occasional 19th-century Utah publication printed in unrecognizable letters and squiggly symbols.

It looks like some sort of secret Mormon code, and in a way, it was.

The letters are from the Deseret Alphabet, a short-lived language conceived by church leader Brigham Young and introduced by territorial Utah's fledgling university in 1854. The idea was to replace the traditional alphabet with one that was more phonetically accurate and easier for Mormon converts arriving from Europe to understand. Critics, however, claimed that Mormons developed the language to shield their writings from outside eyes and isolate them from a world that often viewed them with suspicion.

Young enlisted the help of George D. Watt, a Mormon convert from England who had learned a method of shorthand called phonography. Watt modified English letters and shorthand, and raided his own imagination, to create symbols for thirty-eight different sounds.

Progress was slow, but in 1868 two small primers to the alphabet were published, along with a Deseret Alphabet version of the Book of Mormon. *The Deseret News,* the LDS Church–owned newspaper, printed articles in the new alphabet, and the symbols appeared on coins and gravestones.

But the language never caught on. Most pioneers, busy trying to eke out a living, didn't have the time or patience to learn it. Printing stuff in the new alphabet was expensive. So after two decades of cult use, the Deseret Alphabet died along with Brigham Young in 1877. Today it remains little more than a curiosity for language scholars and Mormon history buffs.

The Ghosts of Topaz

Delta

In the spring of 1942 the desolate desert northwest of town was home only to sagebrush. By the end of that year, it was one of the largest cities in Utah. And by 1946, it was empty again. Even by the boom-and-bust cycles of Western mining towns, this was strange. And Delta is not a mining town.

So what happened? During World War II, the site hosted an internment camp for some 8,000 Japanese-Americans uprooted from their homes by a U.S. government anxious about national security. Called Topaz after a nearby mountain, the camp opened on September 11, 1942, as one of eight major Japanese internment camps in the American West.

Like most towns, it had houses, schools, and a recreation hall. Unlike most towns, it was surrounded by barbed-wire fences and towers patrolled by armed guards who in 1943 shot a 63-year-old man for standing near the fence.

Internees lived in pine barracks with tar-paper walls that provided little insulation against the cold, wind, and dust. Despite these hardships, residents made Topaz into a community. They planted gardens, published a newspaper, staffed a hospital, organized a city government, and formed baseball leagues. After the war ended in 1945 they all left—most returned home to California—and the camp was dismantled.

One camp resident, Harry Yasuda, found work during the war as a typesetter for a newspaper run by Frank Beckwith in nearby Delta. Because of his salary, the U.S. government charged him rent for living in a Topaz barrack.

Today Beckwith's daughter Jane, a Delta schoolteacher, leads efforts to preserve the history of the largely forgotten camp and its residents. She and Utah Japanese-Americans formed a nonprofit organization that has purchased more than 400 acres of the original Topaz site.

Beckwith's group also has launched the beginnings of a Topaz exhibit behind the Great Basin Museum, 328 West 100 North. Their exhibit includes a restored original barrack from the Topaz camp. For more info, call the Great Basin Museum at (801) 864-5013.

Visitors also may drive out to the site of the actual camp itself, 16 miles northwest of town, where some concrete foundations and broken chimneys are all that remain of this brief but shameful chapter of Utah, and American, history.

It's Cosmic, Man
Delta

If someone told you they like to hang out in the desert and study cosmic rays, you might think they smoked too much wacky tobacky back in the Sixties. But that's what scientists do at the Millard County Cosmic Ray Center, a warehouse-like building on the west end of town. Research cosmic rays, that is.

The center is the public face on a new, $17 million cosmic ray observatory that's considered the most powerful in the Western Hemisphere. Scientists hope the observatory will allow them to finally discover the origin of cosmic rays, or ultrahigh-energy particles, that come screaming into Earth's atmosphere from the distant reaches of the universe. Or something like that.

A rare collaboration between universities and institutes in Japan, China, Taiwan, and the United States, the project is expected to begin full operation by fall 2007.

Known as the Telescope Array, the astrophysics project has several major components: three large buildings that house fluorescence detectors—sets of mirrors and recording instruments that scan the night sky for ultraviolet flashes that occur when incoming rays strike the Earth's atmosphere—and 564 table-shaped scintillation detectors resembling solar panels and scattered across miles of desert to measure "air showers," or cascades of subatomic particles that fall to Earth when cosmic rays collide with nitrogen.

Uh, okay. Still with me?

The Telescope Array is expected to conduct research in the desert for at least ten years. To minimize the project's environmental impact on desert ecosystems, the scintillation detectors will be installed by helicopter and maintained by scientists on foot or on horseback.

To have someone explain it all to you properly, visit the Cosmic Ray Center just west of the overpass on Highway 6. The center will house educational exhibits staffed by scientists who actually understand this stuff. Or call (801) 581-6628 or visit www.telescopearray.org.

These panels will fan out across the desert to catch cosmic rays.

Where Have All the Soldiers Gone?

Fairfield

You'd never tell by looking at its two remaining buildings, but from 1858–1861 this hamlet was home to an Army camp that was the largest concentration of troops in the country at the time.

Named Camp Floyd for then-Secretary of War John B. Floyd, the camp held more than 3,500 military and civilian employees sent west by Floyd and President James Buchanan to quell a perceived Mormon rebellion. The costly camp was rumored to be an attempt by Floyd, a known Confederate sympathizer, to drain the federal treasury on the eve of the Civil War.

On a patch of desert along a Pony Express route, the town sprang up almost overnight. Some 400 buildings were hastily erected to accommodate the troops, and enough civilians followed to swell the town to 7,000 people—then half the size of Salt Lake City.

The Mormon uprising never occurred, leaving the soldiers with routine duties that included protecting the nearby overland stage routes, mapping the area, and being bored out of their skulls. Many soldiers spent their pay in Fairfield's seventeen saloons, which attracted gamblers, prostitutes, and other opportunistic characters.

The camp was abandoned when President Abraham Lincoln summoned the troops east to fight the Civil War. Two months after the army left, only eighteen families remained. Today the camp site is a state park with two restored historic buildings: the army commissary, which now hosts a small museum and gift shop, and the Stagecoach Inn, which opened in 1858 and operated for almost a century.

Visitors can tour the former inn. A sign in one of its rooms tells the tale of a frontier-era roomer who was cleaning his gun when it went off, firing a bullet through an adjacent room. The bullet passed seconds after that room's occupant had lain down on the bed, probably sparing his life.

You'll find Camp Floyd and the Stagecoach Inn at 18035 West 1540 North. Just follow the signs. Or for more info call (801) 768-8932.

Desert Diving

Grantsville

What's the last thing you'd expect to find swimming around in a desert hot spring? I'm guessing a shark might be near the top of the list. But Bonneville Seabase, on a remote plain northwest of Grantsville, has several of them—along with hundreds of other tropical ocean fish.

Linda Nelson and husband George Sanders bought the property in 1988 and built a low-slung compound of buildings around the natural-fed springs. The couple run the Neptune Dive store in Salt Lake City and wanted a place to hold scuba-diving classes year-round.

Because of its proximity to the Great Salt Lake, the springs have a salinity content that's comparable to the ocean. And the water is a balmy 80 degrees. So the couple added some warm-weather fish to see what would happen. To their surprise, the fish thrived. They even began breeding.

"Fish aren't nearly as tender as people think they are," says Nelson, who has learned through trial and error what types do best in the strange desert habitat. "They're pretty hardy critters."

Today Bonneville Seabase is home to some sixty tropical species, including angelfish, puffer fish, groupers, pompano, mullet, snappers, and butterfly fish. Oh yes, and a handful of harmless nurse sharks up to 9 feet long. Linda and George import them from all over the world and feed them a daily diet of anchovies, whiting, and squid.

Divers, snorkelers, and even school field trips visit the Seabase weekly to swim among the fish. One of the pools is 60 feet deep, which makes for an authentic ocean-diving experience. Visitors are welcome, and diving gear is available for rent. Just don't be surprised when a shark cruises by.

Bonneville Seabase is open Thursday through Saturday from 9:00 a.m. to 4:00 p.m. and Sunday from 9:00 a.m. to 3:00 p.m. For more information, call (435) 884-3874 or visit www.seabase.net.

The Donner Party Stopped Here

Grantsville

The Donner-Reed party, the ill-fated 19th-century pioneers who fell victim to blizzards, starvation, and cannibalism in the Sierras, are usually associated with California, not Utah. But the travelers' dire fate can be blamed directly on their arduous crossing of Utah's mountains and deserts, which cost them wagons and cattle and delayed them by more than a month, leaving them vulnerable to the Sierras' October snowstorms.

"This desert had been represented to us as only forty miles wide, but we found it nearer eighty," wrote party member Virginia Reed Murphy of Utah in her journal. "It was a dreary, desolate, alkali waste . . . it seemed as though the hand of death had been laid upon the country."

Somehow if Virginia were alive today, I don't think the Utah Travel Council would be offering her a job.

More than a century and a half after the Donner-Reed party passed through what is now Utah in 1846 (the year before the Mormons arrived in Salt Lake City), their wagon tracks are still visible in the salt flats. The group stopped at some natural springs just west of present-day Grantsville. Later, as they battled exhaustion and thirst while crossing Utah's west desert, they abandoned wagons and discarded possessions to lighten their load.

Some of these artifacts are on display in the Donner-Reed Pioneer Museum, which occupies a one-room adobe brick schoolhouse built in

1861. Immediately inside the door you'll find two racks displaying items recovered along the Donner-Reed pioneers' trail: oxen yokes, a rusty Dutch oven, a rifle gun stock, a water keg, a child's shoe, and some broken china. Salt and weather have corroded many of the items, and details about them are sketchy.

Though modest, the museum at 97 North Cooley Lane (300 West) is one of only two in the nation devoted to the Donner-Reed party. It's open seven days a week by appointment only, but curator Claude Parkinson will be happy to let you in. You can reach him at (435) 884-3767, or call city hall at (435) 884-3411.

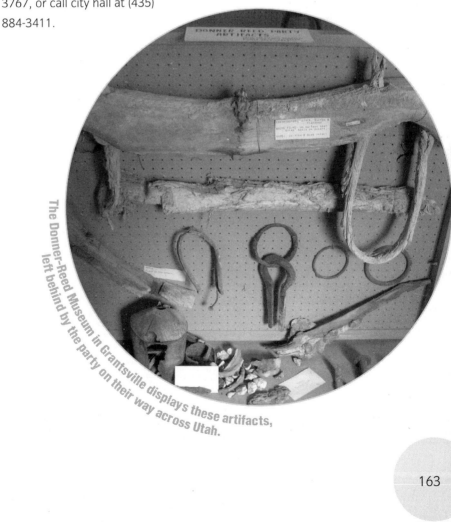

The Donner-Reed Museum in Grantsville displays these artifacts, left behind by the party on their way across Utah.

BOBBING LIKE A CORK

Can you really float like a cork in the Great Salt Lake? Well, yes. The high saline level—three to five times saltier than the ocean—creates a denser form of water that increases buoyancy. Mormon pioneers confirmed this within days of arriving in the Salt Lake Valley in July 1847 when a handful of them, including Brigham Young, ventured to the south shore of the lake and went for a dip.

"Its specific gravity is such to buoy us up in a remarkable manner," wrote one settler about the experience. "We could not get our knees to the bottom but would rise to the top like a cork," wrote another. One bather even climbed upon another in the water but could not sink him.

The lake is salty because it lies in a basin, with no outlet. Streams carry small amounts of salt from the mountains into the lake. After much of the lake's water evaporates, the salt remains.

Dipping a toe in the Great Salt Lake was a popular pastime in the early 1900s, when the Saltair resort drew bathers from miles around. But Utahns rarely do it anymore. Those who venture into the lake find the salt leaves a chalky film on their skin.

If you're determined to go for a salty swim, consider heading to the north shore, above the railroad causeway that bisects the lake. The waters there are even saltier, and more buoyant, than those in the lake's southern half.

Paul Bunyan's Woodpile

Jericho Junction

Paul Bunyan, the giant mythical lumberjack, probably never spent any time chopping trees in Utah. But that didn't stop local folks from naming a peculiar lava rock formation after him.

Formed by volcanic activity some 30 million years ago, Paul Bunyan's Woodpile is a unique geological feature that resembles enormous stacks of cut logs. The formation sits on the lip of a former volcano and was created when magma cooled and cracked into horizontal columns, adding to the "woodpile" effect.

The columns, or "logs," are about a foot wide and up to 15 feet long. Shifting faults in the earth have tilted the piles a little, but they still stand, ready for their namesake to return and build a fire or something.

To see Paul Bunyan's Woodpile, take Highway 6 south from Eureka or northeast from Delta to Jericho Junction, an uninhabited former railroad crossing. The turnoff for the woodpile is 3 miles north of Jericho, on the east side of the highway. Follow a dirt road about 3½ miles to the trailhead, which is marked with a sign. Hike a mile up the trail until you see the woodpile atop the ridge to your left.

Utah's Sandbox
Jericho Junction

If Hollywood ever decides to film a remake of *Lawrence of Arabia,* they won't need to go all the way to Morocco this time. The Little Sahara Recreation Area, a 124-square-mile system of shifting sand dunes, rises like a mirage from the scrubby desert plain surrounding it.

Most of the Little Sahara sand is the result of deposits left by Lake Bonneville 15,000 years ago. After the lake receded, southwesterly winds picked up the exposed sand and dropped it here. The prevailing winds are still pushing the sand dunes to the northeast at a rate of 5 to 9 feet a year—which means Salt Lake City will have a major sand problem in about, oh, 75,000 years.

From this perspective, it looks like a piece of art.

The Little Sahara contains a 9,000-acre nature preserve that's home to mule deer, antelope, horned owls, and nine species of reptiles. Another 60,000 acres are popular with weekend warriors who criss-cross its bowls on dirt bikes, ATVs and, yes, dune buggies. The area's highest point is a 700-foot-tall dune called, fittingly enough, Sand Mountain.

Beside the White Sands Campground and Jericho Picnic Area are two enormous fenced sandboxes. Measuring several acres each, they have enough roaming space to tucker out even the most hyperactive kids.

The entrance fee to Little Sahara is $8 per vehicle. You'll find it 31 miles west of Nephi and just west of Highway 6. For more information visit www.utah .com/playgrounds /little_sahara.

ATV riders love to climb 700-foot-high Sand Mountain.

The Mountain with a Voice

Notch Peak

Notch Peak, a 9,725-foot mountain about 50 miles west of Delta, is believed to be the second-tallest cliff face in America after Yosemite's famed El Capitan. It's also the country's tallest limestone cliff. But that's not what makes it curious.

You see, Notch Peak makes noises. Shifting rock mass deep within the mountain creates rumblings that can be heard for miles, sort of like the moans of some gargantuan beast's empty stomach. Or mine, on a really bad day. The syndicated "Ripley's Believe It Or Not" newspaper column once called it the "Mountain With a Voice."

The same geological phenomenon also is at work in the nearby Drum Mountains to the northeast.

Two trails lead to the top of Notch Peak, offering a dramatic view of the west-facing cliffs that plunge almost 3,000 feet. Vigorous hikers can do the round trip in a day. You can access the trails from the Notch Peak Loop road off of Highway 50.

And if you hear some low, mysterious noises during your hike, you'll know what they are. I hope.

LUAUS IN THE DESERT?

Imagine moving from a lush tropical island to a dry, barren desert, far from civilization, where the summer sun scorches everything in sight and the winters are bitterly cold. Sounds crazy, right?

Well, that's just what hundreds of Mormon converts from Hawaii, Samoa, and other Polynesian islands did in the late 1800s to be closer to the heart of the LDS Church in Salt Lake City. The immigrants established a colony on church-owned land in the desert 75 miles west of Salt Lake City and called it "Iosepa" (pronounced "YO-seppa"), which means "Joseph" in Hawaiian. They named their village after Joseph F. Smith, sixth president of the LDS Church, who served a church mission in Hawaii in the 1850s.

The first Polynesians arrived by wagon in 1889. They built rows of wooden homes, laid out in a traditional Mormon grid system around a square, and installed plumbing, raised livestock, and grew crops. But the harsh weather took its toll on the islanders, who contracted flu, smallpox, and other diseases. Several cases of leprosy even were reported, which isolated Iosepa further from Utahns in Salt Lake City.

That's not what doomed the colony, however. In 1917, the LDS Church built a temple in Hawaii and urged Iosepa's residents to move back to the islands. Within a few years most of them did, abandoning the town they'd spent twenty-eight years building.

Today you'll find the remains of Iosepa along Highway 196, some 15 miles south of I-80. Almost a century later, there's little left of the colony but some old foundations, a monument, and a new pavilion that hosts a Polynesian celebration each Memorial Day weekend. Hundreds of Pacific Islanders come from throughout Utah to dance the hula, roast a pig, and lay flower leis on the graves of their migrant ancestors.

Ophir Heaven's Sake
Ophir

Deer outnumber residents in this slumbering hamlet 7,000 feet above sea level in a narrow dead-end canyon. School buses don't come here because there aren't enough kids to make it worthwhile. Town hall is a one-room building with a wood-burning stove, and the town's fire engine is a Chevy pickup.

With twenty-three residents, give or take a few, Ophir is Utah's smallest incorporated town. There's little need for an official census here, where townspeople identify passing neighbors by the sound of their cars.

Hard to believe that in its heyday a century ago, Ophir was home to some 5,000 miners who lived or camped within town limits. Until it closed in 1973, the Ophir Hill mine produced tons of lead, silver, and zinc—earning the town its biblical name, which means "land rich with gold."

With its weathered cabins and abandoned miners' shacks, Ophir today is but a few cars and people removed from being another Old West ghost town. Long-timers worry the town's population will some-day wither into the single digits. But they don't want to see a flood of newcomers spoil its tranquility, either.

"You're welcome to come on up and visit," mayor Walt Shubert has been known to say. "But don't plan on staying."

Sleep in Utah, Play in Nevada

Route 50, Utah—Nevada border

The Border Inn, a modest motel-cafe-casino complex on desolate Route 50, known as "the loneliest highway in America," has a split personality. The inn sits smack dab on the state line, with the casino ("the fun half") in Nevada and the twenty-nine motel rooms ("the boring half") in Utah.

How appropriate! The two halves are even on different time zones, meaning you can play the slots til midnight, walk 100 feet to your room, and immediately lose an hour. And vice-versa.

Eighty-three miles from the nearest Utah town of any size, the place survives as a gateway to Great Basin National Park and because it's the only oasis around for weary travelers needing a meal or a shower.

But the Border Inn has another little claim to fame: Each January, about 100 aging sheepherders from around western Utah gather here for a casual conference of sorts. Innkeeper Denys Koyle serves them a free dinner of—what else?—lamb, then sets up a microphone so that the old-timers can swap stories about their venerable Old West profession.

Koyle planned on having just one Old Sheepherder's Party, in 2004, but as the evening ended people kept asking her, "You're going to do this again next year, right?" So she did. And again the year after that.

Her only concern? With sheep production on the decline in Utah, there are fewer herders every year. "Ten or fifteen years from now there may not be a sheepherder left in Utah," she says. Let's hope not.

To book a room call (775) 234-7300 or e-mail borderinn@greatbasin park.com.

Bathing? No, but You Can Rock Out

Saltair

Fifteen miles west of Salt Lake City, on the southern shores of the Great Salt Lake, sits a lonely structure with domed spires shaped like Hershey's Kisses and a long history of glory and tragedy.

Planned as a "Coney Island of the West," the first Saltair resort opened in 1893—the product of a partnership between the Mormon Church and a railroad company that shuttled passengers there from Salt Lake City. The ornate Moorish-style pavilion rested on more than 2,000 posts and pilings and lured visitors to float in the lake's briny waters.

In its day the resort had a range of attractions, including a roller coaster, a Ferris wheel, rodeos, bullfights, and hot-air balloons. During its first quarter-century Saltair drew almost half a million visitors a year

In the early 1900s, bathers flocked to Saltair to swim in the Great Salt Lake.

and was for a time considered the most popular family resort west of New York.

Then, in 1925, it burned to the ground. A new Saltair was built the following year, but despite containing what was advertised as the world's largest dance floor, it never regained its former popularity. The Depression sapped business, a 1931 fire caused $100,000 in damage, and drought caused the lake to recede until the shoreline was half a mile away. Later, high winds toppled the roller coaster. After years of struggle, the resort closed its doors in 1958, and it stood abandoned. That didn't stop the Beach Boys from posing before the resort for a 1967 album cover, though.

Fire destroyed Saltair again in 1970. A group of investors built a new, less ornate pavilion in 1981, but rising lake waters flooded the building. New owners restored the structure and reopened it in 1993 as a concert hall. Since then the venue has hosted concerts by scores of pop and rock acts, including the Ramones, Smashing Pumpkins, and the Dave Matthews Band.

Visitors today can walk through the building, which retains little of its historic flavor. But its gift shop sells salt-water taffy and vintage postcards of Saltair's heyday. The resort is accessible by driving west from Salt Lake City on I-80 to the Saltair exit. For more information visit www.thesaltair.com.

Salty Sailing

Saltair

When you hear the phrase, "Yacht Club," you probably think of sport-coat-clad boaters in such preppy harbor locales as Newport, Rhode Island. But Utah's inland sea has the oldest continuously chartered boating club in the nation: the Great Salt Lake Yacht Club, whose motto is, "Home to the World's Saltiest Sailors."

Surprisingly, the Great Salt Lake has proved to be a pretty good place to sail. Because of its high salt content the water never freezes, allowing hardy sailors to venture out on their boats year-round. And because the salt can wreak havoc on engines, only a handful of motorboats use the lake, keeping its waters peaceful.

The first sailing craft to test the lake was the *Mud Hen,* a 15-foot wooden skiff commanded by Mormon pioneers shortly after their arrival in Utah in 1847. By the 1860s, 50-foot schooners were transporting sheep and cattle across the water to graze on Antelope Island. The Great Salt Lake Yacht Club was founded in 1877, the same year one of its sailors launched what is believed to be the first catamaran in the United States.

Because the shallow lake's shoreline swells or falls according to rainfall and drought, low water levels grounded many boats over the decades that followed. Flooding in the early 1980s forced sailors to relocate their boats. But the yacht club persevered, holding regular sailboat races on the lake's salty waters.

Today its members access their boats from a 360-slip marina on the lake's south shore, just west of Saltair from I-80's Saltair exit. The marina is now a state park and is open year-round. For more info on the yacht club, visit www.gslyc.org.

Fire!

Tooele

Are you a firefighter? Would you like to be one? Do you go bonkers for *Backdraft?* Have you seen *Ladder 49* forty-nine times? Then the Utah Firefighters Museum is for you.

Housed in a hangar-like building designed to resemble a fire station, the museum contains more than fifty antique fire engines, pumpers, and trucks dating back to 1914. For added realism, the museum has placed mannequins in firefighter gear inside some of the trucks.

Display cases hold antique nozzles, helmets, uniform patches, and even some charred coins and other mementos recovered from burning buildings. The walls are filled with photos of firefighters in action beside memorabilia such as Dalmatian statues and a framed copy of the poem, "My Grandpa's a Fireman."

C'mon you dummy, we've got a fire to fight!

The museum is maintained by local volunteer firefighters to convey a sense of the honor, dangers, and rewards inherent in their profession. Its exterior courtyard contains a memorial to the more than forty Utah firefighters killed in the line of duty since 1920.

To get there, take Highway 112 west from Tooele until you reach the Deseret Peak Complex. For more information or a guided tour, call (435) 843-4040 or visit www.utahfiremuseum.com.

WANNA WIN A BET?

Spell "Tooele" to a non-Utahn and bet them they can't pronounce the name of this west-desert city that's fast becoming a commuter suburb of Salt Lake City. Offer them five chances. Listen to them wrap their tongue around "Too-ell" and "Too-ee-lee." Then get ready to cash in. The correct pronunciation is "Too-WILL-Uh."

Tell them not to feel bad. Nobody gets it right the first time.

Historians disagree over the origins of the name. Most believe the area is named for Tuilla, a Goshute Indian chief who lived there before the Mormons arrived. Others think the name comes from the tule weed that grows abundantly nearby. Then again, maybe the city founders just wanted to mess with newcomers.

All Aboard!

Tooele

The Tooele Valley Railroad Museum's slogan should be B.Y.O.T., as in Bring Your Own Train. Circling the museum grounds are miniature train tracks—the rails are about a foot apart—and railroad enthusiasts are invited to bring their own customized trains from home, set them on the tracks, and run them around.

Don't have your own train? No problem. Every Saturday, weather permitting, youngsters and adults alike can climb aboard a miniature train that navigates the grounds and even passes through a tunnel.

Trains of all shapes and sizes fill Tooele's railroad museum.

Housed in a former railway station, the museum is a reminder of the days early in the 20th century when miners worked the Oquirrh Mountains east of Tooele. The Tooele Valley Railway transported cargo to and from a smelter 7 miles away in the nearby foothills while serving as a commuter train for smelter employees (fare: 5 cents each way).

The centerpiece of the museum is the railway's 1910 steam locomotive, the last one of its kind in Utah when it was finally retired in 1963. Visitors can climb into the locomotive and do their best Casey Jones impressions.

Also on the grounds are two wood-sided cabooses, a snowplow, and several cars from an antique train once used by the Air Force to transport troops. Inside one of the old Air Force cars is an elaborate HO-scale track running through mountains and villages. Again, visitors are welcome to supply their own trains from home.

The museum is located at 35 North Broadway at Vine Street, 4 blocks east of Tooele's Main Street. It's open Tuesday through Saturday afternoons from Memorial Day to Labor Day. For more information call (435) 882-2836 or (435) 843-2110.

Also in Tooele:

The Benson Grist Mill, a restored historic mill that ground flour and cornmeal from 1854 until the 1940s. The handsome wooden mill is open May through October and hosts a variety of pioneer-themed events. It's located at 325 State Highway 138 (435-882-7678).

It's Tha Bomb

Wendover

Wendover, a gambling town on the Nevada border, draws thousands of Utahns across the salt flats each weekend to its casinos. During World War II, however, the desert town bustled for a very different reason— one that would prove critical to ending the war.

In 1940, with the war escalating in Europe, the Air Force built a base and bombing range just south of town. The military chose Wendover for its isolated location far from people who might get in harm's way, snoop around, or complain about the noise.

This air field doesn't look like much now, but the Enola Gay bombers trained here.

The first training unit arrived in 1942. At its peak a few years later, the base was home to some 20,000 military and civilian personnel and became the largest bomber-training center in the world. Many key bomb groups trained there, including the first squadron to bomb Nazi Germany during daylight.

Wendover became best known, however, as a test and training site for "Little Boy," the atomic bomb dropped on Hiroshima. Col. Paul Tibbets Jr. and the crew of the *Enola Gay* B-29 trained here until leaving for the Pacific to prepare for their mission. Versions of Little Boy were assembled and tested at the bombing range, and the Enola Gay itself was stored in a hangar here for two weeks in June 1945.

During the *Enola Gay* crew's stay at Wendover, the government emphasized the hush-hush nature of their work by posting undercover FBI agents around the base along with signs reading, WHAT YOU SEE HERE, WHAT YOU DO HERE, WHAT YOU HEAR HERE, STAYS HERE. So *that's* where Vegas got its slogan.

The base's colorful history didn't end there. The first unmanned Air Force flight to break the sound barrier occurred over the bombing range. Although the Air Force closed the base in 1963, the historic airfield was later discovered by Hollywood, which shot parts of *Con Air* and *The Hulk* here.

Today a nonprofit group is trying to preserve the airfield's historic character. Still standing are the officers' club, a 60-foot air-traffic-control tower, and some weathered wooden hangars. The base also serves as Wendover's little-used municipal airport. In its operations building is a small museum with historic photos, a display model of the *Enola Gay*, and a helmet and goggles worn by a U.S. airman over Nagasaki.

The airfield also hosts an annual air show each August. To reach the Wendover Airfield, head south from the main strip at the sign just east of the Nugget casino. Or for more info visit www.wendoverairbase.com.

The Flintstones Might Have Partied Here

Wendover

A few miles east of Wendover, down a dirt road, lies one of the most unlikely nightspots you'll ever see. It's not open anymore, but in its day, more than sixty years ago, it was quite the hotspot. Or, in this case, cool spot.

The dance hall is actually a cave at the northern base of Wendover Peak. In the 1940s, airmen stationed at the Wendover Air Base escaped the summer heat by holding dances here. They set up a bar, poured concrete to make a level dance floor, strung lights, and brought in a record player to spin records by Glenn Miller and other big-band acts.

A makeshift officers' club, the spot became known as Juke Box Cave. In addition to keeping the airmen cool, the natural rock walls and ceiling served another useful purpose—they kept light from bleeding out of the cave at night and violating the wartime blackout.

When the war ended in 1945, so did the dances. To deter vandals from looting the cave of its ancient Indian rock art and other archeological treasures, state officials fenced off its opening in the 1990s. They also fenced off nearby Danger Cave, in which scientists in the early 1950s found evidence of Utah's first inhabitants, who occupied the cave some 10,300 years ago.

If you still want to see the caves for yourself, take exit 4 off I-80, head north half a mile, and then turn left on a paved road that eventually becomes a dirt road. Follow it to Wendover Peak; both caves are located on the mountain's east side.

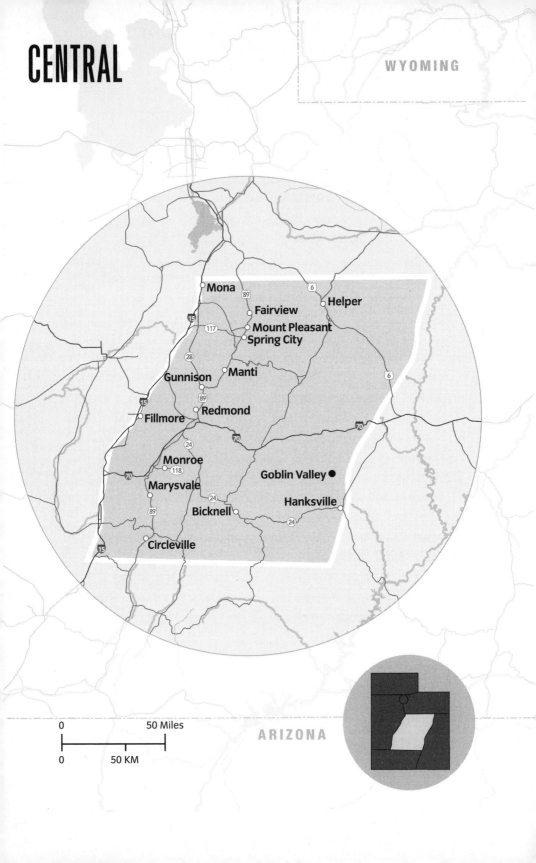

CENTRAL

WYOMING

Mona
89
6
Fairview
Helper
15
117
Mount Pleasant
Spring City
28
6
Manti
Gunnison
15
89
Redmond
70
Fillmore
70
24
70
Monroe
118
Goblin Valley ●
Marysvale
70
24
Hanksville
89
Bicknell
24
15
Circleville

0   50 Miles

0   50 KM

ARIZONA

CENTRAL

So when was the last time you had a slice of pickle pie? Or sipped a glass of dandelion wine? Or saw the spot "where the bluebird sings to the lemonade springs?" Central Utah, with its fertile valleys dotted with little farm towns, looks like a conventional enough place. But the folks who live here know how to get goofy.

Witness Mount Pleasant's annual rhubarb festival, which turns otherwise sane folks into Rhubarbarians. Or the Bicknell International Film Festival, which celebrates trashy B-movies and invites attendees to participate in the world's fastest parade. Or Fillmore's ATV Jamboree, where kid riders compete in bathtub races and get spattered in mud bogs.

Here you can see Butch Cassidy's boyhood home, sleep where Zane Grey slept, soak in some hippie-run hot springs, drool over the Big Rock Candy Mountain, see a shrine to one of the longest-married couples in history, visit what may be the largest lavender farm in the world, peer inside a "hollow mountain," and explore an alien-planet-looking valley full of cute little rock goblins.

Oh, and I haven't forgotten about the pie. So bring your appetite. Right this way, please.

Bad Movies and the World's Fastest Parade

Bicknell

Nobody will ever confuse the Bicknell International Film Festival with Sundance or Cannes. For one, Bicknell attracts no movie stars. The "international" thing is a joke. And the festival premieres no new films—only classic B-movies from the past, such as *Attack of the Killer Tomatoes.*

Organizers launched BIFF in 1996 as "the smallest international film festival in the world." Although attendance has grown since then, there's little evidence to dispute the claim. Bicknell is a town of about 350 people in a remote valley near Capitol Reef National Park. Festival films are shown at the town's—heck, the county's—only cinema, the single-screen Wayne Theatre on Bicknell's sleepy Main Street. Attendees number in the low hundreds, and there's plenty of free parking.

That's exactly what cult film director Trent Harris (*Rubin and Ed*) and Lory Smith, who co-founded what became the Sundance Film Festival, had in mind when they launched BIFF. Both wanted to create a tongue-in-cheek antidote to the crowds, paparazzi, and pretension of festivals they'd attended elsewhere.

Each year, BIFF organizers build the festival slate—usually three films—around a theme. The first year, it was space-alien movies like *The Day the Earth Stood Still*. Since then they've done mutant-insect movies (*Earth vs. the Spider*), troubled-teen movies (*High School Confidential*), '60s beach movies (*Beach Blanket Bingo*), and even circus movies (*Big Top Pee Wee*).

The festival's slogan, printed on its T-shirts, is "Where Good Things Happen to Bad Movies." Each year organizers offer BIFF's annual Wayne Award to singer Wayne Newton, but he has yet to show up to collect it. Other festival traditions include a swap meet, a party or two, and the "World's Fastest Parade," a 55-mph convoy of decorated vehicles that make the 8-mile trek to Bicknell from neighboring Torrey.

"The first year [of the parade], we kind of got in trouble because we didn't exactly tell the police what we were doing," says festival co-organizer James Anderson, who runs the Wayne Theatre with his wife Sue. But Anderson says that law enforcement and other local folks have since come to embrace the eccentric event as "something weird but fun."

The Bicknell International Film Festival is held each year on the third weekend in July. For more information visit www.waynetheatre.com.

The Pie Queen of Wayne County
Bicknell

Any down-home cafe worth its salt serves a good apple or cherry pie. But buttermilk pie? Oatmeal pie? Pinto bean pie? Pickle pie?

These unorthodox but surprisingly tasty creations have been a staple at the Sunglow motel-restaurant since the late 1960s, when owner Cula Ekker founded the place. Cula's pies were on the menu from the beginning, and folks began coming from miles around just for a bite. Some customers were known to skip their entree and go straight for a slice, baked by the acknowledged "Pie Queen of Wayne County."

Cula doesn't work in the cafe anymore; in 1997, she sold the business to its current owners, Ronnie and Patty Krause. Before hanging up her apron Cula passed on her recipes to Patty, who faithfully reproduces them daily. In those early transitional days Cula even visited the cafe every day to help Patty get the pies just right.

"She still checks on us a lot," Patty says.

Today, some forty years after Cula opened her cafe, her famous pie recipes live on. Cula's "secret" pickle pie recipe even hangs, framed, on the restaurant wall. In case you're wondering, pickle pie is made with sweet pickles, cinnamon, and nutmeg (among more basic things, like sugar), and tastes a little like mincemeat pie.

The most popular pie, however, is the pinto bean, which tastes kinda like pecan pie. Patty won't reveal that recipe just yet. "If someone wants it bad enough, they'll have to buy the whole place," she says.

The Sunglow restaurant serves breakfast, lunch, and dinner six days a week and pie anytime (they make an apple pie, too). The adjoining motel, built in a classic 1960s style, has fifteen clean, comfortable rooms—perfect for sleeping off a pie-eating binge. Visit it at 91 East Main Street (435-425-3701) or at www.sunglowpies.com.

Young Butch Cassidy
Circleville

Butch Cassidy's legacy is everywhere you look in these parts. If he were still alive, he'd probably shake his head in bemusement at it all—then saddle up and ride off into the hills. Visitors to Circleville, where the outlaw lived as a boy, will find a Butch Cassidy antiques store, the Butch Cassidy Hideout Motel and Café, and the Butch Cassidy Rodeo Days, held each August.

It's funny to see all these tributes to a man who, in his day, was notorious for robbing banks and trains. I guess Hollywood, and Paul Newman, can confer cool on anybody.

If you visited Circleville in 1880 and asked for Butch Cassidy, folks would greet you with blank stares. He was then known as Robert LeRoy Parker and lived with his Mormon-convert parents in a one-room cabin just south of town. Young Roy, as his folks called him, worked at ranches across southwestern Utah before falling under the spell of a charismatic local rogue named Mike Cassidy.

Enamored with the nomadic outlaw lifestyle, "Roy" eventually adopted Cassidy's name. The "Butch" nickname reportedly came later, when the bandit worked briefly as a butcher in Rock Springs, Wyoming.

The rest you probably know: Cassidy and a band of elite robbers called the Wild Bunch—including Harry "Sundance Kid" Longabaugh—spent the next two decades roaming the West, rustling cattle, and robbing banks. To ease their getaways, they stashed a series of fast horses along their escape routes, allowing them to elude their pursuers by galloping for hours.

As a boy, Butch Cassidy lived in this tiny cabin with his family. No wonder he left home as soon as he could.

For years legend held that Butch died in a shootout in Bolivia in 1908. But when *Butch Cassidy and the Sundance Kid* became a hit in 1969, reporters descended on Circleville to interview Cassidy's younger sister, Lula Parker Betenson, who told them that her famous brother returned to Circleville for a family visit in 1925 and later died of natural causes in Spokane, Washington, at age sixty-eight. Some historians now believe Cassidy faked his death in Bolivia and spent his last years living quietly and lawfully in America.

Whatever happened to Butch, there's no denying the existence of his boyhood home, which still stands on private property in a grove of poplar trees. Its owners have considered turning the tiny weathered cabin into a museum but have settled so far for restoring it instead.

You can't go inside the unmarked historic cabin. But you can get a clear view of it from Highway 89. Head just south mile marker 156 and look west across a hayfield. Or just ask anyone in town for directions.

Butch Cassidy

Here's to the Happy Couple

Fairview

A golden wedding anniversary? That's nothing. A seventy-five-year diamond wedding anniversary? Piece o' cake. A Fairview couple, Peter and Celestia Peterson, were hitched for eighty-one years and ten months—making them one of the longest-married couples in American history.

Their marriage began in St. George in 1878, when they were both eighteen, and ended only with Peter's death at one hundred in October 1960. Celestia died a year later at the age of 101.

We owe our eighty-one-year marriage to love — and my violin.

On their seventy-fifth anniversary, the town of Fairview held a day in their honor; on their eightieth, they got a telegram of congratulations from President Eisenhower. Their years together landed them in the pages of *Life* magazine in 1959, although their record was eclipsed in 2004 by a Rhode Island couple married for eighty-three years.

The Petersons are honored with a "Shrine to Love and Devotion" inside the Fairview Museum of History and Art, whose eclectic collection includes everything from prehistoric skeletons to ornate hand-woven lace to a diorama display of miniature horse-drawn carriages and coaches. The Peterson display includes newspaper clippings and a life-size sculpture of the couple by Avard T. Fairbanks, a Utah artist known for crafting the Angel Moroni sculptures that crown the spires of several Mormon temples.

The museum contains some ninety sculptures, including a series depicting Abraham Lincoln at various stages in his life, by the late Fairbanks, a Provo native whose work is on display at the U.S. Capitol in Washington, D.C., and around the country. You'll find it open year-round at 85 North 100 East (435-427-9216).

A Short-Lived Capital

Fillmore

Imagine if America's founding fathers, when choosing a city in which to locate their new country's capital, had snubbed Washington, D.C., in favor of a small town in Kansas. That's sort of what happened in 1850s territorial Utah, when Brigham Young and other Mormon leaders bypassed Salt Lake City as capital for the more geographically central hamlet of Fillmore—population, oh, several dozen.

Fillmore, named by Young for then-U.S. President Millard Fillmore to curry favor with the federal government during Utah's campaign to become a state, lies 148 miles south of Salt Lake City. As pioneer law-makers soon found out, it was a long haul by stagecoach.

Original plans for the territorial statehouse called for four wings connected by a large dome at the center. The presumably flattered President Fillmore procured enough funds to build the statehouse's south wing. Construction stalled, however, after Fillmore lost the next election and funding dried up. But the stoneworkers' initials are still visible on the building's exterior walls.

Undaunted, the territory's fledgling legislature held its 1855 session in the handsome stone building. It was to be the only one. The next year, and for every year afterwards, lawmakers convened instead in the relative metropolis of Salt Lake City.

After falling into disrepair, the abandoned statehouse was restored in the 1920s. Today it stands as the oldest existing government building in the state and hosts a museum full of period artifacts. Its top floor

Portraits of grim-faced pioneers line the basement walls of Utah's former capitol.

holds the assembly hall where the legislature met so briefly, while the walls of the basement's corridor are lined floor to ceiling with portraits of unsmiling pioneers.

The basement also houses a jail cell complete with an ankle chain anchored to the stone floor and a list of rather dated jailable offenses, including "unlawful horseback riding."

The museum is open year-round and is located behind the county courthouse on Main Street. Admission is $2. For more information, call (801) 743-5316.

Shopping, Taxidermy, and Marilyn, Too

Fillmore

The Pioneer Market is sorta like a small-town Wal-Mart, only with stuffed wild animals. A one-stop-shopping mix of groceries, outdoors gear, and assorted taxidermy, the store sells, as *The Salt Lake Tribune* once noted, "everything from buttermilk to buckshot."

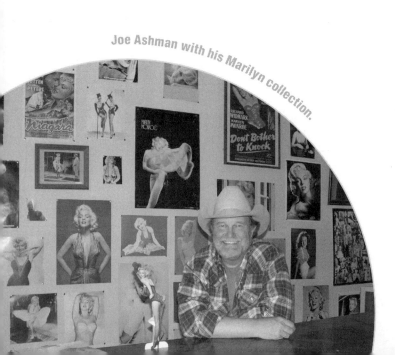

Joe Ashman with his Marilyn collection.

As you might guess, owner Joe Ashman is a hunter. The first clue is the large rack of elk antlers mounted on the historic brick building's roofline above its front door. The storefront display windows contain a stuffed bear and another elk—whole this time. More stuffed critters, like the bobcat in the potato chip aisle, are scattered throughout the store. A sign on the wall near the rifle display reads, GOD, GUNS & GUTS MADE AMERICA. The most interesting part of the store, however, is the upstairs, where Ashman presides over a garage sale–like hodgepodge of antique guns, Western memorabilia, and antiques. Head towards the back and you'll find an adjacent room whose walls are covered with hundreds of photos and posters of Marilyn Monroe. You might say Joe has a bit of a crush on the late movie star.

"My wife told me I could have one other woman," he says, "As long as she was dead."

On a nearby shelf are dozens of Marilyn books, videos, and other collectibles. Joe says he'd sell his entire Marilyn collection for the right price, but you get the feeling he'd miss her if she were gone.

You'll find the Pioneer Market, and Joe, at 10 South Main Street or call (435) 743-5355.

Also in Fillmore:

The annual National ATV Jamboree, which brings riders from around the West to navigate hundreds of miles of mountain and desert trails. The event, held in late June, ends with an ATV parade down Main Street and a mud bog, which lets riders get down and really dirty. For info call (800) 441-4ATV or visit www.atvutah.com/fillmore.

HERE A MAMMOTH, THERE A MAMMOTH

If you do enough museum-hopping around Utah, you'll probably see the 20-foot-high skeleton of a prehistoric mammoth, an ancestor of the modern elephant, at the Utah Museum of Natural History in Salt Lake City. You also may notice the mammoth looks a lot like another one at the Fairview Museum of History and Art. Come to think of it, the mammoth also is the spitting image of a third skeleton at the College of Eastern Utah's Prehistoric Museum in Price.

What's going on here? Was Utah really such a hotbed for these big-tusked creatures 15,000 years ago?

Well, yes—and no. As you may have guessed, all three are life-size cast replicas of the same skeleton, found in 1988 in the mountains above Huntington by workers repairing an earthen dam. (The actual bones are in storage at the CEU museum in Price.)

The discovery was remarkable for several reasons: The mammoth was found at 9,000 feet above sea level, a record-high elevation for what was a plains animal. And 98 percent of the skeleton was intact, almost perfectly preserved in the near-frozen mud.

After analyzing the remains, scientists determined the mammoth was a sixty-five-year-old bull whose last meal was a batch of fir needles—a poor diet for anyone, let alone an elephant. As he lay down for his last nap, the old fellow could never imagine that he'd one day be cloned—in triplicate.

Mammoths, mammoths, everywhere.

The World's Biggest Jungle Gym

Goblin Valley

Imagine cresting a desert ridge and discovering a hidden valley filled with thousands of curious, gnome-like rock formations. That's what happened in the late 1920s to Arthur Chaffin, who was searching for a shortcut between Caineville and Green River when he and two companions stumbled across such a place.

Fascinated with the squat, toadstool-like shapes, Chaffin called it Mushroom Valley. Not bad for a first try. But, maybe because no mushrooms grow within miles of the arid place, the name never stuck. The Utah government designated it Goblin Valley State Park in 1964, and the whimsical little valley has enchanted visitors ever since.

Sculpted by wind and water over millions of years, its sandstone shapes conjure thoughts of otherworldly creatures. Indeed, the lunar-like surface doubled for an alien planet in the 1999 Tim Allen movie *Galaxy Quest*.

Hundreds of mushroom-shaped rock gnomes greet visitors to Goblin Valley.

The park is especially popular with kids, who scurry between and clamber atop the goblins in elaborate games of tag and hide-and-seek. It's also a great place to tell ghost stories under a full moon, when the goblins cast eerie shadows.

The park contains picnic areas, campgrounds, restrooms, and several hiking trails. To reach Goblin Valley, turn west from Highway 24 between Hanksville and Interstate 70. For more information call (435) 564-3633 or visit www.stateparks.utah.gov.

A Short-Lived Zion in the Desert

Gunnison

On a desolate knoll 3 miles southwest of Gunnison rest two solitary graves, their tombstones inscribed in both English and Hebrew. The weathered stone markers are among the last remnants of a failed experiment: a colony of Jewish transplants who hoped to escape urban poverty by farming in rural Utah.

The colony, known as Clarion, was born in 1911 after sparsely populated Utah began advertising for settlers and selling its land cheap. Some 150 Russian Jews from Philadelphia and New York took the state up on its offer, coinciding with a worldwide "back to the soil" movement that encouraged Jews to seek a simpler life in the country.

The first Jews arrived at Clarion in the fall of that year, attracting stares from Gunnison residents as they rode through town in an open wagon, singing Ukrainian folk songs. They quickly cleared brush, plowed the earth, and planted crops. By the fall of 1912, the colony had grown to twenty-three families, and Utah's governor journeyed 135 miles from Salt Lake City to attend its first harvest festival.

But the settlers' success was brief. The soil was poor, their water supply was unreliable, and they lacked the know-how to create a proper irrigation system. Because almost none of the Jews had farming experience, such basic tasks as harnessing a horse were a mystery. The fields did not produce enough crops to allow the immigrants to repay their loans on the property, and the state of Utah foreclosed after four years.

The colony's wood-frame houses were sold at auction and moved elsewhere. Most of the colonists returned to the East Coast, although a few hung on in Clarion until the 1920s. The only traces of Clarion left today, besides the graves, are some worn concrete foundations and the remains of a collapsed cistern.

To visit Clarion, head west from Gunnison on 100 South and follow the street as it curves south and becomes a dirt road. Keep going until you see the weathered foundations.

Hollow Mountain Gas & Go

Hanksville

Never underestimate a man with a dream—and some dynamite.

In the early 1980s miner Harry Thompson noticed traffic passing through this tiny town on the way to Lake Powell and thought it might make a good place for a gas station and convenience store. Trouble was, Harry wanted to stake his claim at the junction of Highways 24 and 95, on a spot covered by a sandstone hill.

With his background as a miner, Harry figured he could remove enough of the rocky mound to build his store. So he drilled holes in the rock, dropped in dynamite, and started blasting away. After a while Harry realized it would be easier to locate the store inside his man-made cave than to keep blasting.

He named his enterprise Hollow Mountain, although "mountain" is a generous term for what looks to be about a 60-foot hill. It opened shortly before Easter in 1984 and was an immediate success with travelers seeking gas, a cold drink, a T-shirt, or fish bait from the little gift shop. During heavy storms, however, rain would run off the rock and into his front door.

Although Harry fitted his hollowed-out store with a tiled floor, walls and a ceiling, you can still see sections of the exposed cave walls—especially back by the restrooms, which are accessed through a cave-like rock arch.

Harry sold his venture in 2004 to current owner Don Lusko, but Hollow Mountain lives on. Lusko enjoys the novelty of running a one-of-a-kind business and hopes to expand, if his rock driller holds out.

"You don't have to paint the place. Or shingle it," he says with a chuckle. "Because the roof doesn't leak."

It's darn near impossible to miss Hollow Mountain as you pass through Hanksville—just look for the sign with the big red arrow, affixed to what may be the world's smallest mountain. Or call (435) 542-3298.

Hollow Hill might be more like it.

THE UNKNOWN FATHER OF TV

Does the name Philo Farnsworth mean anything to you? Maybe not—he died in Salt Lake City in 1971, little known and penniless. But sports widows everywhere might curse him, if only they knew who he was: Farnsworth was the first person to demonstrate and patent a working electronic television system.

Farnsworth was born in 1906 on a farm near Beaver and rode to school on horseback. By the time he was six, he announced to his parents that he wanted to be an inventor. When the family moved to Rigby, Idaho, Farnsworth found a stash of technology magazines in the new house and became fascinated with electronics.

While plowing his father's field, Farnsworth hit upon the idea for how to scan an image and turn it into an electrical signal that could be transmitted. He was fourteen. Excited, the boy scribbled a diagram on a high-school blackboard to show his chemistry teacher how it worked.

After attending BYU and attracting funding for his research, Farnsworth developed a camera tube that transmitted its first image, a straight line, at a laboratory in San Francisco. About the same time, electronics giant RCA was close to developing its own TV technology. RCA president David Sarnoff visited Farnsworth's lab and offered him $100,000 for his work. The inventor turned him down.

By the 1930s RCA and its lead inventor, Vladimir Zworykin, had developed its own camera tube. Soon Farnsworth and the company were locked in a legal battle over who should be awarded the patent for television. A key witness in the case was Farnsworth's chemistry teacher, who reproduced the boy's original drawing of his design.

The U.S. Patent Office awarded the patent to Farnsworth. But he never received fair payment for his work, and RCA, thanks to its corporate muscle, got most of the credit. Many scientists refused to believe that a farm boy and college dropout could have possibly done what Farnsworth did. Disheart-

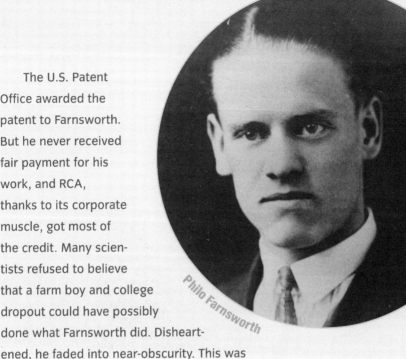

Philo Farnsworth

ened, he faded into near-obscurity. This was underscored in 1957 when Farnsworth appeared on the TV show *I've Got a Secret* and panelists failed to identify him.

But thanks in part to his widow, Elma Farnsworth, who worked tirelessly to earn recognition for her late husband, Farnsworth's legacy has made a comeback. The U.S. Postal Service honored him with a stamp in 1983. In 1999, *Time* magazine named him one of the 20th century's greatest scientists.

Ironically, Farnsworth didn't care for much TV programming, although he told his wife that watching live coverage of the 1969 moon landing "made it all worthwhile." Statues of Farnsworth sit today in the U.S. Capitol and outside the courthouse in Beaver. And the Oquirrh Mountain peak where Salt Lake City's TV antennas sit is named for him. Not bad for a farm boy.

Big John

Helper

They don't call him Big John for nothing. This towering statue of a miner, erected in the 1960s in front of the Helper Civic Auditorium, stands over 20 feet tall. An average-size adult standing beside him comes up to his knee.

Big John towers over ordinary-sized folks.

John wears a miner's helmet, carries a pickaxe, and is painted a shiny black as a symbol of the area's coal-mining roots. His name is believed to come from Jimmy Dean's 1961 hit song, "Big Bad John," about an enormous coal miner who saved his fellow workers from a collapsing mine by holding up a sagging timber until they escaped. Big Bad John then died in the cave-in.

Big John the statue is less of a hero, seeing how he just stands there peering over downtown Helper. But he sure looks impressive. You can see him twenty-four hours a day at 19 South Main Street. Or just ask anyone in town.

Claims, Trains, and a Historical Feel

Helper

As musty old attractions go, the Western Mining and RR Museum is one of the best. How many museums have a coin-operated G-scale train that circles an elaborate western scene over and over for only 25 cents? Or a simulated coal mine in the basement, complete with black "rock" walls, timber supports, and canaries in a cage?

OK, so they're not live canaries, but you get my point.

Located in a former hotel, this venerable museum has room after room filled with displays and artifacts from Carbon County's early-1900s heyday as a coal-mining and railroading center of the West. Each room is devoted to a different aspect of pioneer mining life, from bootlegging to schooling to the thousands of Italian immigrants who settled here. Over the museum's four floors you'll find a doctor's office, a nursery, a kitchen, a beauty shop, a company store, and a room dedicated to the coal-camp baseball leagues.

Among the more notable artifacts are a fossilized dinosaur track recovered from a mine, safety signs printed in multiple languages for

the many immigrant miners, grape-crushers and stills used during Prohibition, some 1930s–era counterfeit coins, and an antique "electric
permanent wave machine" used in a local beauty parlor.

Also on display are the actual steps from a coal-company office in
nearby Castle Dale, which Butch Cassidy and his gang robbed of $7,000
in miners' payroll in 1897. I know, I know—*the steps?* But hey, Butch's
boots trod them, and you take what you can get.

On a more serious note, the museum also contains displays on Utah
mine explosions that killed more than 400 miners in the past century.

Behind the museum is an outdoor display of antique mechanized
mining equipment. The gift shop sells historic photos, Butch Cassidy
posters, engineers' caps, and statues
made from coal. The museum is
open year-round at 296
South Main Street. For
more information call
(435) 472-3009.

Mining equipment, like this old cart, is on display outside the
Western Mining and RR Museum in Helper.

WHAT'S IN A NAME?

Levan, a little town about ninety minutes' drive south of Salt Lake City, has a normal enough name, I guess. But the name's origins are somewhat of a mystery. Some folks say Brigham Young dubbed the town after a friend. Others, maybe as a joke, say Young gave the town its name in a more indirect manner while on an overnight trip with some of his wives: Fed up with the disgruntled Ann Eliza Young (who later divorced him), the Mormon Church president allegedly halted his party in the area to rest and decided to "leave Ann." But the best explanation of all may be that Levan, which sits squarely in the state's midsection, spells "navel" backwards. Says mayor Bob Shepherd, "That probably makes for a better story than the truth."

Utah's belly button?

Eight Nights of Miracles

Manti

What annual Utah event combines a cast of hundreds, tens of thousands of spectators, the Book of Mormon, and lots of bug repellent? The Mormon Miracle Pageant, a free religious spectacle that attracts more than 100,000 spectators over eight nights, making it what is believed to be the largest outdoor theatrical production in the country. Since its debut more than forty years ago, more than 4.2 million people have seen it.

The pageant began in 1967 as a one-night show in a rodeo arena. It now unfolds every June on a hillside below Manti's illuminated Mormon temple, which towers over the town like a white fairy-tale castle. Performances begin at dusk under powerful spotlights, and audience members—the vast majority of them Mormon—spread out on blankets or folding chairs on the lawn at the base of the hill.

"This is the story of the Mormon miracle," says a narrator to open the show, his amplified voice booming over the crowd. A volunteer cast of more than 800 then enacts scenes from the Book of Mormon, the life of church founder Joseph Smith, the pioneer trek across the plains, and the completion of the Manti Temple in 1888.

Taped narration tells the story, mixed with Mormon scripture, while actors lip-synch their lines and use broad gestures visible from the back row hundreds of yards away. Scenes unfold to recorded music by the Mormon Tabernacle Choir. The show ends with hundreds of white-robed men and women greeting a newly deceased character in heaven. By then there's barely a dry eye in the house.

Manti hosts the pageant each year around the time of the summer solstice. For more information visit www.mormonmiracle.org.

UTAH'S ODD GEOGRAPHY

The Uintas are the only major mountain range in the contiguous United States that run east-west. The range contains more than a thousand natural lakes, the largest wilderness area in the state, and 13,528-foot Kings Peak, the highest mountain in Utah. The Uintas also are home to Camp Steiner, the nation's highest Boy Scout camp, at an elevation of 10,400 feet.

The Bear River, which meanders for some 500 miles, is the longest river in the Western Hemisphere that does not eventually flow into an ocean. The river begins in the Uintas of northeastern Utah, flows into Wyoming, back into Utah, into Wyoming again, and then through southeastern Idaho before returning to Utah and into the Great Salt Lake.

The Great Salt Lake, despite being twice the size of Rhode Island, is never more than 30 feet deep.

Each of Utah's twenty-nine counties has a mountain peak over 9,000 feet high, and most are taller than 11,000 feet. This consistency means the average elevation of the tallest mountain in each Utah county is 11,222 feet—a figure higher than any other state, even Colorado and Alaska.

A 106-acre stand of quaking aspen trees in the Wasatch Mountains holds the title of the world's largest living plant. Why? The trees, estimated to be a million years old, share a single root system.

You've Heard the Song, Now See the Mountain

Marysvale

Usually, places inspire songs. Here, however, it happened the other way around.

The song in question is "Big Rock Candy Mountain," a turn-of-the-twentieth-century hobo ballad first made famous by Harry McClintock, who recorded it in 1928 under the name Haywire Mac. A hobo fantasy of sorts, the lyrics describe the mythical mountain as a wondrous place where trees are made of cigarettes and a "bluebird sings" at the "lemonade springs."

After the song's release, a group of Marysvale residents got themselves a laugh by placing a sign at the base of a colorful local peak and naming it Big Rock Candy Mountain. They also erected another sign proclaiming a nearby stream Lemonade Springs. To their surprise, the names stuck, and tourists began journeying to see the places named in the song.

OK, so the mountain doesn't look much like rock candy. But its treeless ridges and gullies, visible from the road below, are various shades of red, yellow, orange, and white—the result of volcanic mineral deposits.

A Utah couple, Ben and LaRue Dieringer, opened a Big Rock Candy Mountain resort at the base of the mountain and ran it from the 1930s until the 1960s. The song gained new popularity in 1949 when Burl Ives recorded it and again in 1960 when a third version hit the charts. Many folks today know it from yet another version, which appears on the *O Brother, Where Art Thou?* soundtrack.

Although the Dieringers are long gone, the Big Rock Candy Mountain resort still operates today. It features cabins, a cafe, and a gift shop that sells rock candy and sheet music to the song.

The mountain and the resort are located along Highway 89, about 8 miles south of I-70.

Can you see the big rock candy on this mountain? Me neither.

Well, If It's Good Enough for Butch and Zane . . .

Marysvale

Moore's Old Pine Inn, Utah's oldest operating hotel, is one of many places in the state celebrated for sheltering outlaw Butch Cassidy on his travels. But the Pine Inn has another distinction: It also hosted famous Western author Zane Grey, who reportedly wrote at least part of *Riders of the Purple Sage* here.

The hotel was built in 1882 (as if to prove its venerability, editions of *The New York Times* from 1878 are still glued to the rafters). It originally catered to gold miners and prospectors who flocked to the area's mines in the late 1800s. Legend has it that Butch Cassidy spent a night at the hotel before busting a buddy out of the jail across the street.

The building hadn't functioned as a hotel for some twenty-five years before Randy and Katie Moore bought it in 1994 and restored it to something like its former glory. Guests now can stay in one of seven themed rooms, including the Zane Grey room, whose shelves hold some seventy of his books.

The miner's suite contains a replica of a mine shaft, while the fishing room has a 20-pound stuffed bass over the bed. Behind the original inn is an Old West–style annex with more rooms, including a "brothel" room with a red light outside its door.

You'll find Moore's Old Pine Inn at 60 South State Street. For reservations call (435) 326-4565 or (800) 887-4565.

Also in Marysvale:

Access to the Paiute ATV Trail, considered one of the finest and most famous in the country. The 260-mile loop passes through Marysvale and three mountain ranges and climbs to 11,000 feet above sea level in places.

The remains of Old Bullion City, an 1868 mining town in a canyon just west of town. Now called Miners' Park, it contains old mine portals, a mill, cabins, and some restored mining equipment.

Lavender Fields Forever
Mona

If you visit the town of Mona in June or July, you'll notice acres of irrigated desert blooming with purple blossoms—a brilliant display of color not unlike the summer fields of southern France. *Qu'est que c'est?* You're looking what may be the largest lavender farm in the world.

Young Living Lavender Farm is the brainchild of D. Gary Young, an Idaho native who says he discovered the healing powers of essential oils in 1973 after a tree fell on him, paralyzing him from the neck down. Through years of treatment with natural medicines—especially essential oils—Young says he eventually learned to walk again and even ran a half-marathon in 1986.

Although some doctors doubt the veracity of these claims, there's no denying the success of Young's vision. After first growing aromatic herbs on a quarter-acre farm in Eastern Washington in 1989, Young moved his farming operation to Mona and built Young Living Essential Oils into a thriving multilevel marketing company. Young Living now distills its home-grown herbs into hundreds of consumer products, from soaps and skin lotions to nutritional supplements, that are sold around the world.

Along the way, he turned the Mona farm into an eclectic theme park with an herb garden, paddleboat pond, rock-climbing wall, Old West frontier town, and even a medieval arena that holds jousting matches. The farm's biggest event is Lavender Days, a two-day festival in early July that includes herb planting and cooking classes, distillery tours, and a 5k run through the blooming lavender fields.

To visit Young Living Lavender Farm, turn off Interstate 15 at exits 233 or 242, head west, and follow the signs. For more information call (800) 371-0819 or visit www.younglivingfarms.com.

Mellow Out and Have a Soak, Man
Monroe

Utah is full of natural hot springs, but there's not another quite like the Mystic Hot Springs, an unlikely hippie hotbed—hotpool?—in a town that otherwise wouldn't see many of them.

The artesian springs bubble out of the foothills above town at a rate of more than 150 gallons per minute and have been popular with locals since the days when Indians would soak in them and decorate their bodies with the red mud. Water emerges from the ground at a scalding temperature of 168 degrees, leaving minerals that build up over time into glistening mounds of red rock. (Don't worry—the two large soaking pools and eight bathtubs are a more human-friendly 110 degrees.)

Today the springs are owned by Mike Ginsburg, a graphic artist who helped design animation for video screens used by the Grateful Dead during their summer tours in 1991 and 1992. In his day he also designed enough different Grateful Dead stickers to cover a VW bus.

Mike was heading home to Denver after a Dead show in Las Vegas in 1995—the year Jerry Garcia's death broke up the band—when he stumbled across what were then called the Monroe Hot Springs. Enchanted

Mystic Hot Springs owner Mike Ginsburg and friend beside his soaking tubs.

with the property and the view of the Sevier Valley from the hot pools, he bought the place, hauled in some old pioneer cabins for guests, and turned it into a ramshackle resort. A resort with an abandoned swimming pool, teepees, drum circles, and six naturally warm ponds stocked with tropical fish.

Since the late 1990s Ginsburg also has made his resort a regular stop for the many Dead-influenced jam bands that crisscross the West. Each year Mystic Hot Springs hosts concerts by such bands as Leftover Salmon, which Mike records on videotape and posts on the resort's Web site, www.mystichotsprings.com. Fans come from miles around to hear the music, camp on the property, and soak in the springs.

Such gatherings conjure images of drug-fueled hippie orgies. And Monroe's townspeople will tell you they feared exactly that. But Mike says his resort policy against drugs, alcohol, and nudity has so far kept things from getting out of hand.

The resort is open twenty-four hours, which is good to know if you're in the area and get a hankering for a hot-spring soak at 2:00 a.m. Campsites, hot showers, and RV hookups are available, as are a handful of restored cabins, which rent for $50 a night. All fees include access to the hot springs. A soak in the springs without an overnight stay will cost you $7.50.

To reach Mystic Hot Springs, turn east on 100 North off Monroe's Main Street and head east 5 blocks. For more info visit the Web site or call (435) 527-3286.

If It Grows on a Tree, They'll Make Wine from It

Mount Pleasant

Although church doctrine prohibits Mormons from drinking alcohol, some of Utah's early Mormon pioneers were known to make, and imbibe, their own wines from local fruits. In that spirit, Bob Sorenson and Carolyn "Winnie" Wood opened their tiny Native Wines winery in 1999, making mostly grape-free wines you'd never find in the Napa Valley.

Working from a historic former butcher shop, Bob and Winnie age their wines in oak barrels, glass carboys, and stainless-steel drums. Their methods are self-taught, based on research, trial and error, and experimenting with lots of different hand-picked fruits and flowers: apples, pears, plums, figs, cranberries, currants, honeysuckle, quince, rosehips, gooseberries, huckleberries—even dandelions and rhubarb, for cryin' out loud.

The couple makes wine from wild berries, neighbors' excess ripening fruit, and their own orchards, which grow apricots, cherries, pears, and more than a dozen varieties of heirloom apples.

The wines are for sale through the winery or by special order through Utah's state liquor stores. The winery is open six days a week, although visitors are urged to call ahead (435-462-9261) for tasting appointments. Native Wines is located at 72 South 500 West in Mount Pleasant, just off Highway 89.

It's Rhubarbaric

Mount Pleasant

Where will you find the Queen of the Rhubarb, the Defender of the Rhubarb, and a Rhubarbarian all at once? Why, the Sanpitch Rhubarb Festival, of course.

Celebrated the third Saturday of May since 2000, the event marks the spring harvest of a Sanpete Valley native crop: the humble rhubarb plant. Festivities range from the expected (a rhubarb pie–eating contest) to the offbeat (an Ugly Truck Parade, with a trophy awarded to the ugliest) to the downright goofy (the Turkey Trot, at which contestants bet on where they believe a wandering turkey will relieve itself).

"There's nothing serious about this," says event organizer John McClellan. "It's just a whimsical kind of thing."

Festivalgoers nibble on rhubarb muffins, rhubarb salsa, rhubarb ice cream, and "rhu-burgers" while sipping rhubarb soda and rhubarb wine. People come dressed as rhubarb stalks, kids race custom-built carts in a Soap Box Derby, and spectators cheer as a fleet of synchronized riding mowers parade down the street (don't ask).

Meanwhile, the winner of the uncooked rhubarb-eating contest is crowned the festival's Rhubarbarian. Oh, how they rue the barbs they must get from their friends.

For more info about the Rhubarb Festival call (435) 462-9261.

A pie-eating contest is part of the fun at Mount Pleasant's annual Rhubarb Festival.

Well, Back to the Salt Mines
Redmond

When folks first see Redmond sea salt, they think it's harvested from evaporated ocean water. Then, after they notice the Redmond company is based in landlocked Utah, they assume it's scooped from the salt flats near the Great Salt Lake. But the grainy white stuff actually comes from this small town, some 200 miles south of the briny lake, that is home to Utah's only underground salt mine.

Geologists believe the salt was deposited during the Jurassic period about 150 million years ago, when an inland sea covered the area. After the sea dried up and left a salt basin, volcanic forces deep within the earth pushed a huge salt dome, almost 5,000 feet deep, to the surface.

Legend has it that the Fremont Indians first discovered the salt deposits here centuries ago when they noticed deer eating the soil. But nobody harvested the salt until the 1960s, when several drought-stricken farmers turned to salt mining to make a few extra bucks.

Today Redmond, Inc. burrows 3 miles into a mountain to extract half a million tons annually of rock salt for de-icing roads, salt blocks for live-stock, and, yes, table salt under the RealSalt brand. Unlike most table salt, which has been bleached white, RealSalt contains colorful specks of such minerals as calcium, potassium, sulphur, iron, copper, iodine, and zinc. Tastes pretty good, too.

The Redmond folks offered public tours of the mine until the federal government, concerned about safety, made them stop. Tourists today can still watch the above-ground mining operations, view a forty-minute video about the mine's history, and visit the company gift shop. Because you never know when you may need a few bags of road salt, for the road.

The Redmond salt mine is located just north of town at 6005 North 100 West. For more info call (866) 735-7258 or visit www.redmond natural.com.

CAN'T YOU HOLD IT FOR ANOTHER 100 MILES?

Here's a bladder-busting fact: The 105 remote miles of I-70 between Salina and Green River is the longest stretch of highway without services in the federal interstate system. That's right: No gas stations, no fast-food joints, no motels. So plan accordingly.

There is a rest area with toilets, however, at mile marker 85. Whew!

Take a Pot, Leave a Dollar (or Ten)

Spring City

You'd never find a shop like Horseshoe Mountain Pottery in the big city. For starters, owner Joe Bennion welcomes visitors to stop by and chat while he's spinning clay on the wheel or firing pots in his kiln out back. And when Joe's not around, he leaves the front door open. Shoppers are free to come in; select what they want from his showroom of pots, plates, mugs, and bowls; and leave their payment in a metal box.

"I haven't locked this door in twenty years. I don't even know where the key is," says Joe, who shrugs off his mother's fears that he'll get robbed. "If I had a liquor store, it'd be a problem. But pottery—it's hard enough for me to sell it."

That's the kind of simple, small-town lifestyle Joe and his wife, painter Lee Bennion, wanted when they moved to this historic burg in 1977 after meeting in the art department at Brigham Young University. They bought the 1890s building—a former grocery store—on Spring City's quiet Main Street, raised three daughters, and pursued their art. Joe named his pottery shop for Horseshoe Mountain, a crescent-shaped ridge southeast of town.

Dozens of other artists followed the Bennions to Spring City, one of the best-preserved historic towns in the West, creating a picturesque enclave of artisans, painters, violin-makers, and at least one potter. One of the best-known artists in Utah, Joe is the subject of *The Potter's Meal*, a short film that played at film festivals around the country.

When they're not creating pottery, Joe guides river trips while Lee rides horses and sells Mom's Stuff, a healing salve she makes with herbs from her garden. They also run a popular Web site full of family news, updates on their art, and personal musings about the rewards of small-town life.

So come by anytime. Joe won't mind. "I'm used to throwing [clay] and talking at the same time," he says. "It's kind of like an act that I do."

You'll find Joe and Lee at 278 South Main Street. If you want to call ahead, the number is (435) 462-2708.

Joe Bennion welcomes visitors to his pottery shop.

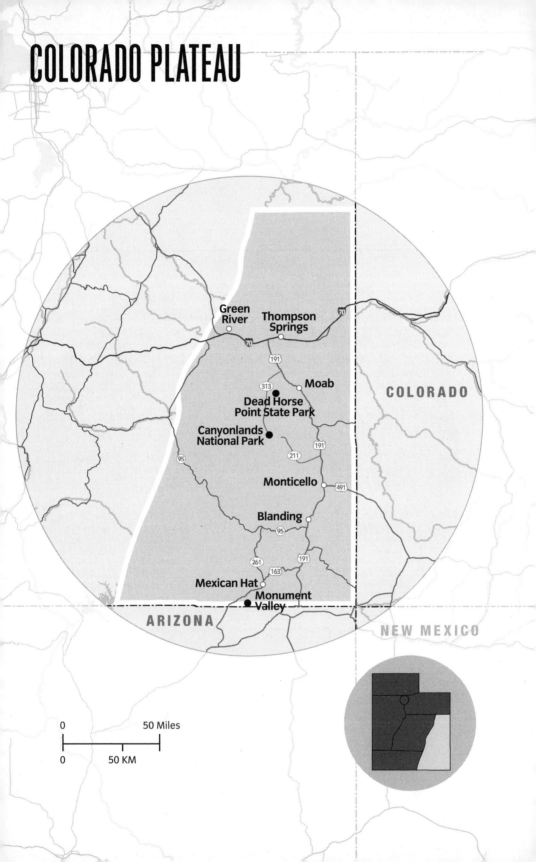

COLORADO PLATEAU

Green River

Thompson Springs

70

70

191

313

Moab

Dead Horse Point State Park

Canyonlands National Park

191

211

95

Monticello

491

Blanding

95

261

191

163

Mexican Hat

Monument Valley

COLORADO

ARIZONA

NEW MEXICO

0   50 Miles

0   50 KM

COLORADO PLATEAU

This part of Utah, carved by time and the winding Colorado River, is what the West is all about: untamed and awesomely beautiful. Its postcard landscapes—from red-rock cliffs to raging whitewater to snow-capped peaks to towering spires of stone—make almost anywhere else pale in comparison.

Some of these places are so rugged and remote that they were among the last in the continental United States to be discovered and mapped. And with names like Dirty Devil River, Robbers Roost Canyon, and Valley of the Gods, they even sound cool.

If the canyons and buttes around these parts look like something from a John Ford Western, well, that's no coincidence—he filmed his movies here. Combine that Hollywood legacy with the Navajo reservation that covers the state's southeast corner, and you've got cowboys *and* Indians.

The Old West, come to life—but in color this time.

Start your visit in Green River, home to a river-rafters-themed tavern, a balky 60-foot geyser, and the biggest melon on wheels you've ever seen. Watch for falling rock at gravity-defying Landscape Arch, which you'll swear is due to collapse, like, *any minute*. Then head south through Moab, the mining boomtown-turned-mountain-biking Mecca, to tour a fourteen-room home blasted out of a cliff.

Keep going past Newspaper Rock, past Satan's Speedway, past a museum that celebrates dinosaurs as scientific marvels *and* movie stars. Here's where the scenery starts getting really crazy. You can detour up the thousand-foot cliffs of the Moki Dugway or keep heading south to Monument Valley, with its famous buttes. Ten minutes here and you'll understand why the Navajos consider this place sacred.

Riding shotgun along the way will be the ghosts of such colorful figures as Butch Cassidy, one-armed John Wesley Powell, cantankerous Georgie White, mysterious wanderer Everett Ruess, John Wayne, and yes, even Forrest Gump.

Ready to roll? You won't be disappointed.

T-Rex, Please Report to Makeup

Blanding

There are dinosaur buffs, and then there is Stephen Czerkas. The native Californian sculpted his first dino from mud when he was four. At age eight, he used his parents' video camera to make a brief stop-motion dinosaur film. In his twenties he built dino models for a low-budget sci-fi flick, *Planet of the Dinosaurs.*

It won't surprise you, then, to hear that Czerkas and his equally dinosaur-obsessed wife, Sylvia—they met at a "Dinosaur Society" potluck dinner—operate Utah's only dinosaur museum that celebrates the extinct creatures both as scientific marvels and as movie stars.

Their Dinosaur Museum, which opened in 1994, showcases many of the Czerkases' remarkably lifelike, full-size models of raptors, T-Rexes, and other toothy critters. It also contains such rare dinosaur-related items as a four-billion-year-old meteorite from Namibia and several petrified logs from the Permian period, some 275 million years ago.

But the museum's most unusual feature is its impressive collection of dino pop-culture memorabilia, including hundreds of dinosaur comic books, pulp novels, action figures, and boxes of breakfast cereal. One

Blanding's Dinosaur Museum.

Who says dinosaurs can't be comic-book heroes?

long hallway is lined with vintage posters from dozens of dinosaur-themed movies, from the 1925 silent classic *The Lost World* and the first *King Kong* to such B-movie spectaculars as *Reptilicus*, *The Giant Claw*, and *The Beast of Hollow Mountain*.

Yup, you'll even find a poster for *Planet of the Dinosaurs*.

The Dinosaur Museum is open April 15 to October 15 at 754 South 200 West. Admission is $2. For more information call (435) 678-3454.

The World's Biggest . . . Salt Blob?

Canyonlands National Park

One of the most intriguing hikes in the national park system leads to an enormous circular rock formation that appears to be a vast crater. Upon closer inspection, however, it more closely resembles a massive dome with a huge hole in its roof, sort of like an NFL stadium. A 2-mile-wide NFL stadium.

Called Upheaval Dome, the enigmatic structure has long fascinated scientists who suspect it wasn't built by ancestral Puebloan Indians centuries ago to host sporting events.

So how was it formed?

Many researchers believe the domed crater was created when a meteorite ⅓-mile wide crashed into southeast Utah between 5 million and 100 million years ago. Ooooh. (Not the same meteorite that wiped out the dinosaurs, however.) They suspect the top layer of the crater later eroded away, exposing the dome, which formed when the ground rebounded from the impact.

In 1995 a team of NASA scientists spent $150,000 on a study to determine what created the bizarre bulge. They even thumped the ground over and over with a 700-pound weight to create seismic waves. Their conclusion? Upheaval Dome is the impact crater left by a stray comet or asteroid. But several years later, another study by a group of Texas geologists determined that that the crater was formed not by a flying projectile from space but by something equally sci-fi movie-like: a salt blob.

That's right. The study found that a ½-mile-wide blob of salt erupted to the surface from a thick underground salt layer roughly 200 million years ago, produced a pancake-like "salt glacier," and then eroded somewhat after the salt disappeared.

It's too bad the two groups can't agree on what happened so the park service can erect some new signs. Because while Upheaval Dome sounds interesting, it's no match on paper for the Meteor Crater or the Salt Blob.

The Upheaval Dome is located in the Island in the Sky section of Canyonlands National Park. The trail from the parking lot to the rim of the domed crater is about a third of a mile.

Sad Story, Great Views
Dead Horse Point State Park

Dead Horse Point is a rocky promontory whose steep cliffs plummet 2,000 feet on three sides to the Colorado River below. On the fourth side, a narrow neck of land provides the only escape off the mesa.

As you might guess, there's a story behind the point's name. In the frontier days of the late 1800s, herds of mustangs ran wild on the nearby mesas. Cowboys used the point as a natural corral into which they would drive the wild horses. The neck, which is only 30 yards wide, was then fenced off.

The finer horses were roped and broken there on the point, while the rejects, called "broomtails," were left to wander off through an open gate in the fence.

According to legend, one group of broomtails was abandoned on the point to find their way back to the open range. But even though the gate was open, for some reason the mustangs remained on the arid point and died of thirst—in plain sight of the river below.

Today the point is a Utah state park with campgrounds, picnic areas, a visitor center and, best of all, a spectacular view. But if you visit the park with a horse-loving child, you might want to skip telling them the story behind its name.

You can visit Dead Horse Point State Park by turning west off Highway 191 north of Moab and driving 18 miles. Admission is $7. For more info visit www.utah.com/stateparks/dead_horse.

Eat at Ray's

Green River

No eastern Utah river-running trip is complete without a visit to Ray's Tavern, a legendary rafters' hangout with famous burgers, cheap beer, and more than a hundred boaters' T-shirts on the walls.

The bustling tavern sits in the middle of this otherwise quiet town, a popular starting point for rafting expeditions on the Green and Colorado Rivers. Ray's has sat in its current location since 1947 and is such an institution among rafters that some have held wedding receptions here. The remains of a bowling alley and a roller rink are still visible in the basement, which was also rumored to be a secret hangout for Edward Abbey's fictional Monkey Wrench Gang of environmental anarchists.

Ray's menu is basic—mostly pizza and burgers, cooked on a corner grill behind the worn wooden bar. To discourage more exotic orders, the place once offered a peanut-butter-and-jelly sandwich for $75. Longtime regulars reminisce about former waitresses with names like Mumbles, Pickles, and Radar.

Old wooden booths line the wall of the main bar, while a back room holds a pool table and a jukebox full of country music. Ray's most distinctive feature, however, are the 130 framed rafters' T-shirts that line the walls. Many of the shirts came off the backs of boaters fresh from the Green River, while rafters from around the country donated others from as far away as Alaska. Some of the wittier shirts read, "Sclerosis of the River," and "Shitfer-branz Expeditions."

Ray's is located at 25 South Broadway. They don't take reservations, but if you want to call anyway, the number is (435) 564-3511.

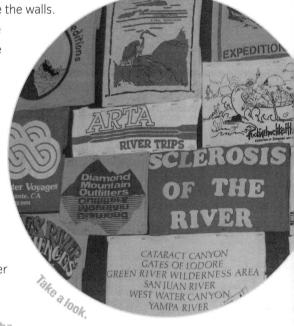

Take a look.

At Ray's, the burgers are matched only by the cleverness of the river-rafting T-shirts on the walls.

Now That's One Big Melon

Green River

Lots of towns across America call themselves watermelon capitals. But how many can boast a "Big Slice," a 25-foot-long chunk of melon on wheels (or should that be "mel-on wheels?") that's the highlight of Green River's annual Melon Days festival.

Green River wasn't always a green melon town. Settled because of its riverside location on an overland mail route, the town had brief flurries of railroad and mining activity before local residents discovered agriculture. In the early 1900s settlers planted several hundred acres of peach trees, but the harsh winter killed them before they could bear fruit.

As J.H. "Melon" Brown soon discovered, however, melons proved hardier that peaches. A cash crop was born, and a town developed its identity as the melon capital of the state. Today Green River's cool nights and hot summers produce fine watermelons, cantaloupes, and

The Big Slice is a highlight of Green River's annual Melon Days parade.

even a hard-skinned "winter melon" that keeps until Christmas. In the late summer and fall roadside melon stands pop up all over town.

In 2006 Green River celebrated the 100th year of its Melon Days, a harvest festival held the second weekend of September. It features music, crafts booths, people wearing melon hats, and all the free watermelon you can eat.

Of course, there's also a parade down Main Street. The parade's featured attraction is the "Big Slice," which is crafted from wood and painted to resemble a watermelon, seeds and all. The Slice is mounted atop a truck frame with an engine; a driver sits inside the hollow melon and steers by peering out of a tiny hole.

City employee Roy Pfander has driven the Big Slice in recent Melon Days parades and will tell you it's no easy task. "It broke down a couple of years ago on Main Street and we had to push it," he says.

For more about Green River's Melon Days call (435) 564-3448 or visit www.greenriverutah.com.

Green River is Utah's melon capital.

Brave or Crazy?

Green River

John Wesley Powell was many things: soldier, naturalist, geologist, explorer. One thing he was not, however, was a coward. After commanding Union troops in the Civil War, Powell led the first-ever passage down the Green and Colorado Rivers and through the Grand Canyon, a treacherous 1,000-mile journey over uncharted rapids in leaky wooden boats.

After a three-month trek so arduous that three of his men quit midstream, Powell did it again. And did I mention that he accomplished this with only one arm?

Powell's famous 1869 trip opened up the last unmapped area of the continental United States and impressed even the region's Native Americans, who considered navigating the Grand Canyon gorge impossible. He commanded the pioneering expedition lashed to a wooden chair atop his lead boat, named the *Emma Dean* as a possible appeasement to his worried-sick wife.

"What falls there are, we know not; what rocks beset the channel, we know not," Powell wrote before departing. The hazards of the journey were driven home within three weeks when one of the wooden boats split in two at fierce rapids Powell named Disaster Falls. (Luckily, the men's three-gallon keg of whiskey was saved.) Later Powell got trapped on a ledge while climbing some cliffs above the Green River. He was rescued by one of his men, who climbed to a ledge above Powell, took off his pants, and lowered them for Powell to use as a rope.

Many times Powell and his men were forced to carry their boats overland around waterfalls. By the journey's final days, they were weary, sun-blistered, and subsisting almost entirely on coffee. Their loved ones feared they were dead. But Powell and five other men emerged from the canyon alive that summer to make history. (Two other boatsmen, weary of the river, deserted the expedition several days earlier and were killed by Indians.)

A century later Lake Powell was named after him—a dubious distinction, considering Powell may have been dismayed to see the canyons he traversed flooded by billions of gallons of water.

Powell's remarkable story is recounted at the John Wesley Powell River History Museum, aptly located on the banks of the Green River at 1765 East Main Street in Green River (435-564-3427). Among its attractions are a twenty-two-minute film about Powell's expedition, a replica of the doomed boat *No Name*, and several dramatic sculptures depicting the boatmen battling turbulent rapids.

Would you run the raging Colorado in a wooden boat? John Wesley Powell did.

"THE THOREAU OF THE AMERICAN WEST," BUT CRANKIER

There will never be another Edward Abbey, and south-eastern Utahns of all stripes could probably debate for hours on whether or not that's a good thing. A cantankerous environmentalist author known for his criticism of public-land policies, he once wrote an essay whose narrator tossed beer cans out of his car, claiming that the highway had already ruined the landscape.

Abbey's first famous book, *Desert Solitaire,* was based on the journals he kept as a seasonal ranger in the late 1950s at Arches National Monument (now a national park) outside Moab. The book reveled in the red-rock wilderness of the Southwest and decried the human forces threatening it, including tourism.

In one of its best-known passages Abbey writes, "Do not jump into your automobile next June and rush out to [Utah] hoping to see some of that which I have attempted to evoke in these pages. In the first place you can't see anything from a car; you've got to get out of the goddamned contraption and walk, better yet crawl, on hands and knees. . .when traces of blood begin to mark your trail you'll see something, maybe."

Later he caused a ruckus with 1975's *The Monkey Wrench Gang,* a comic novel about a colorful band of anarchists who conspire to blow up Glen Canyon Dam, the massive concrete structure on the Colorado River that created Lake Powell. Although Abbey said the book was intended as satire, critics argued it advocated eco-sabotage.

Indeed, the book helped inspire radical environmentalists such as the Earth First! Group, whose members pulled stunts like sitting in trees to thwart loggers. It also probably got Abbey a secret file at the FBI.

Larry McMurtry once called him "the Thoreau of the American West." But Abbey loathed being pigeonholed. He had little use for political correctness, supported the National Rifle Association, and angered folks on the left almost as much as folks on the right.

Ed died in 1989 at age sixty-two. A rebel to the end, he left detailed instructions on how he wanted to be buried: No undertakers, no coffin. Just an old sleeping bag, buried somewhere remote and secret in the desert. A brief, simple ceremony with some music and gunfire. His friends honored his requests, burying him in an anonymous spot in Arizona. Then, according to his wishes, they had a raucous wake, filled with drinking, dancing, chili, and corn on the cob.

Old Faithful, It's Not

Green River

Old Faithful, the famous geyser in Yellowstone National Park, earned its name by erupting like clockwork some twenty times a day. Scientists can predict when it'll blow, within a ten-minute window, 90 percent of the time.

The Crystal Geyser, a little-known waterspout 7 miles south of Green River? Not so much.

This unpredictable geyser was created in the 1930s when speculators were drilling for mineral deposits in the area. One drill hole didn't yield any valuable minerals, but it produced something much cooler: a fountain that erupts daily, up to 60 feet in the air.

Most geysers are a product of geothermal activity far beneath the earth's surface and produce scalding water. The Crystal Geyser, on the other hand, is a rare cold-water phenomenon that is powered by pressured carbon dioxide gas. Unlike Old Faithful, its waterspouts can last more than an hour.

Now, about that eruption schedule: Nobody seems to have one. Some observers say the geyser blows every twelve to sixteen hours or so; others say it's more like every five. People do seem to agree that it's slowing down, though. So bring a picnic and lawn chairs—it's gonna be a wait.

To get to the geyser head east from downtown Green River on Main Street and go south on Hasting Road. Pass underneath Interstate 70, turn left at the T-stop, and go about 2 miles to an intersection. Turn right and go 4 miles to the geyser, which lies on the banks of the Green River.

Someone has installed a steel pipe at the base of the geyser, and the surrounding rock is colored a rusty orange from mineral deposits in the water. Be patient: The geyser can bubble for quite a while before it finally bursts.

A Town Named for a Rock

Mexican Hat

Mexican Hat is a quiet town of less than a hundred people on the banks of the muddy San Juan River. It's little more than a stopover for tourists on their way to or from Monument Valley, but it's got a couple of things going for it: The river, which winds through a picturesque rocky canyon.

And its name, of course.

Mexican Hat got its name from this rock, shaped like an upside-down sombrero.

The hamlet is named for an unusual rock formation above the river just north of town. Perched precariously atop a little bluff is a large circular rock that resembles an upside-down sombrero. The brim measures 60 feet across and looks like it could topple in a windstorm.

Legend holds that the peculiar formation was created by an old medicine man who turned a Mexican youth, or at least his hat, to stone after a local maiden took a shine to him.

To visit the rock head north on Highway 163 from town and turn right at the sign. Mexican Hat Rock is a few hundreds yard down the road. Bring some chips, salsa, and margaritas and make a fiesta of it!

The Scariest Road in Utah?

Mexican Hat

You can drive all over the West, but you'll never find another road quite like the Moki Dugway. Considering the steely nerves required to navigate its unpaved cliff-face turns, maybe that's a good thing.

Part of State Highway 261, the gravel dugway is a series of sharp switchbacks that snake their way down—or up, depending on which way you're going—the sheer rock cliffs of Cedar Mesa to the Valley of the Gods below. That's an elevation drop of a thousand feet in 3 miles, without guardrails. No wonder one travel writer calls it "the roller-coaster ride of Southern Utah."

A relic of the Cold War, the dugway was built in the 1950s by the Texas Zinc Minerals Corp. so that ore from a mine atop Cedar Mesa could be hauled to a mill near Mexican Hat. No ore-laden trucks traverse the dugway anymore, and large trailers are discouraged, but you'll still see drivers in RVs white-knuckling it down the road.

As you approach the Moki (also spelled Mokee) Dugway from the north you'll notice a series of ominous yellow road signs announcing SHARP CURVES, STEEP GRADE, NARROW GRAVEL ROAD , and 1,100 FT. DROP NEXT 3 MILES. Well, you can't say you weren't warned. When you reach the dugway—defined basically as a road dug out of a cliff—the asphalt gives way to dirt and the speed limit drops to 5 mph to prevent reckless motorists from pulling an inadvertent "Thelma & Louise."

Climbing the dugway has its reward, though: A spectacular view of mountains, cliffs, and rock spires spanning four states.

You'll find the Moki Dugway 7 miles north of Highway 261's intersection with Highway 163. Warning: Driving the dugway is not recommended during snow or rainstorms, when the road gets muddy and treacherous.

You can drive down a cliff on the Mokee Dugway.

The Valley of the Gods

Mexican Hat

In most parts of America, the term "bed-and-breakfast" conjures images of a quaint restored Victorian home in a historic tourist town, a short stroll from shops and restaurants. But the Valley of the Gods Bed & Breakfast is neither Victorian nor within a long stroll of anything—except some of the most spectacular scenery you've ever seen.

"We're the only building in 360,000 acres," says Claire Dorgan, who runs the remote place with her husband Gary. "You really feel like you've stepped into a John Wayne movie. You almost expect Indians to come over the horizon. It's literally one of the last places in America where you can see nothing."

Or everything. From the B&B's front porch on a clear day you can see 100 miles into Arizona, Colorado, and New Mexico, not to mention Monument Valley some 25 miles to the south. The ranch also lies in the shadow of the towering 1,000-foot cliffs of Cedar Mesa, a few miles to the west.

Like Monument Valley, its more famous neighbor, the Valley of Gods contains dramatic sandstone spires rising hundreds of feet from the desert floor. Unlike Monument Valley, it's almost completely uninhabited. A 17-mile loop on a dirt road takes you past stony pinnacles with names like "Battleship Rock," "Lady in a Tub," and "Seven Sailors Butte," named because it resembles a row of men in sailor caps.

The B&B occupies a stone ranch house 12 miles from the nearest building. It was built in 1933 by the grandchildren of John D. Lee, the pioneer who operated Lee's Ferry across the Colorado River and was later shot by a firing squad for his role in the infamous Mountain Meadows Massacre.

Its four rooms are comfortable in a rustic way and cooled in summer by stone walls more than 2 feet thick. Electricity comes from solar panels and a windmill; gas comes from propane tanks; and water is trucked in from Mexican Hat, 12 miles away. And phone lines? Forget it. The Dorgans field calls on a cell phone with a Colorado number because that's where the nearest cellular tower is.

"We're completely off the grid," Claire says with a chuckle. "There is no grid here."

The Valley of the Gods B&B is open year-round. Rates are $135 per couple, which includes a full breakfast. For reservations call (970) 749-1164.

Also in Mexican Hat:

The Mexican Hat Lodge, whose outdoor, Western-themed restaurant features a grill that swings back and forth over an open fire. Thus its motto, "Home of the Swinging Steak." It's on the main drag (Highway 163), across from the Shell station (435-683-2222).

Near Mexican Hat is the Four Corners Monument, erected to mark the only point in the country shared by four states: Utah, Arizona, Colorado, and New Mexico. Visitors can step onto the granite-and-bronze monument, get down on their hands and knees, and straddle all four states at once. To access the monument head southeast from Aneth on Highway 262 and follow the signs. Admission is $3.

ROBBER'S ROOST

Between the Colorado and Dirty Devil Rivers lies a rugged stretch of desolate country carved with deep canyons and pocked with hidden washes. Known as Robber's Roost, this forbidding terrain became a late-1800s hideout for Butch Cassidy and his Wild Bunch of bank robbers, train robbers, and cattle rustlers.

Nobody seems to agree on exactly where in this vast area Butch and his gang hung out. Maybe that's because the Roost, one of several remote refuges on the north-south route that became known as the Outlaw Trail, was never successfully raided by the authorities despite several attempts.

Cassidy and his crew of outlaws retreated to the Robber's Roost after a Colorado bank robbery in 1889 and again after a mining-company payroll heist in 1897. As the legend of the Wild Bunch grew, so did that of the Roost, which gained a reputation for being impregnable.

One bandit wrote Utah Gov. Heber Wells from prison that the Roost was defended by a 200-man army with plenty of guns and an intricate network of fortifications, tunnels, and land mines. No wonder law enforcement wasn't exactly aggressive about investigating.

The fabled Robber's Roost has inspired a handful of Utah landmarks, including a Green River motel and a Torrey bookstore. In the finest tribute, however, one of the Dirty Devil's tributaries east of Hanksville is now called Robber's Roost Canyon. Enter it at your own risk.

Hole n" The Rock

Moab

Drive 12 miles south of Moab on Highway 191 and you'll come upon a huge red sandstone monolith beside the road. This wouldn't be unusual—southern Utah is full of huge red sandstone monoliths—but for the words painted across its face in big white letters: HOLE N" THE ROCK. Hmm. How can you not stop for a look?

To be honest, "Hole" is an understatement. For what's n' the rock is actually more like a fourteen-room apartment, sculpted cavelike out of the rocky dome as if by some modern-day descendant of Michelangelo and Fred Flintstone. A one-of-a-kind, 5,000-square-foot apartment that once served as a home to the man who built it.

Let me explain.

Albert Christensen grew up beside the monolith with his four brothers in a one-room cabin so small the family slept outside in tents. So no

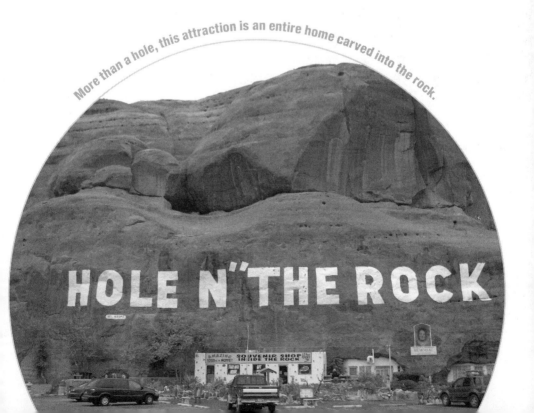

More than a hole, this attraction is an entire home carved into the rock.

wonder when it came time to build a house of his own, Albert wanted something a little roomier. Albert drew inspiration from his father Niels, who was the first family member to see the rock's potential as a dwelling. Using old mining tools and dynamite, Niels Christensen hollowed out a little cave in the 1920s that became a bedroom for the boys.

As a young man, Albert learned to sculpt while serving a prison term for bootlegging. Upon his release, he returned to the family homestead by the rock, where he and his brothers blasted out more space and opened a diner. For several years, it was a local hotspot, with liquor and dancing. After the diner closed, Albert met Gladys Davis, a Colorado woman who expressed interest in his cave-dwelling project.

FRANKLIN D. ROOSEVELT
MEMORIAL
Created and Sculptured
By Albert L. Christe...

A bust of Franklin D. Roosevelt lies in this alcove near the entrance.

Good thing, because it soon became their home. The couple moved into the place in 1952. By this time, Albert and his brothers had expanded the diner to include living areas, bedrooms and bathrooms separated only by thick rock pillars. They lay carpet, imported furniture, strung wires for electricity, and used a drill to bore a 60-foot chimney for the rock fireplace. Because the massive rock maintains a near-constant temperature of 65 to 70 degrees, a heating system was not needed.

The couple maintained a restaurant at the "hole" for several years, with Albert as the chef. When the mining boom subsided and business waned, Gladys opened a gift shop. And whenever Albert needed a little more closet space, he just got out his pickaxe. Albert died in 1957 and is buried in a rocky cove east of the entrance; Gladys joined him there in 1974.

In 2000 Gladys's son Hub sold the Hole N' the Rock to Erik and Wyn-dee Hansen, who continue to operate it as a tourist attraction. More than 50,000 visitors a year take the ten-minute guided tour through the Christensen's old home, whose interior has been preserved just the way it was when the couple lived there.

Inside the "rock" are many of Albert's and Gladys's personal relics, including Albert's original oil painting of himself as Jesus, a taxidermied burro, and Gladys's doll collection. Outside, a mini Mount Rushmore–like head of Franklin Roosevelt (carved by Albert, who was an admirer) sits in an alcove near the entrance. Also on the property are a trading post, a rock garden, a general store, a yard full of quirky statuary, and a little zoo with ostriches and wallabies.

Hole N' the Rock is open seven days a week, year-round. Guides offer tours of the home several times an hour; admission is $5 for adults. For more information call (435) 686-2250.

It's Delicate, So Don't Mess with It

Moab

You've seen it in pictures. It's on a postage stamp and Utah's centennial license plate. The Olympic torch relay passed through the rock span on its way to the Salt Lake City Games in 2002.

A freestanding natural rock arch in Arches National Park, Delicate Arch is an internationally known landmark and the unofficial state symbol. Perched precariously near a steep chasm at the end of a popular 1½-mile trail, it attracts hikers and photographers almost daily. Because of its bow-legged shape, cowboys called it "the Chaps" and "the Schoolmarm's Bloomers" before Frank Beckwith named the arch officially in 1934.

I'm still a little partial to Schoolmarm's Bloomers Arch, myself.

What you may not know is that Delicate Arch also has a recent history as a controversial target for photographers and climbers. In 2000, professional nature photographer Michael Fatali led a workshop to the arch to demonstrate "nighttime photographic techniques."

Fatali used Duraflame logs to set fires underneath the arch and create dramatic lighting for his photographs. But aluminum pans failed to contain the fires, which left sooty residue and scorch marks on the sandstone. Fatali was convicted of defacing federal property and ordered to pay the National Park Service to help clean up his mess. But some of the stains remain today.

In May 2005 a 34-year-old professional climber named Dean Potter made national headlines by scaling the arch. His climb touched off a storm of criticism from climbers and conservationists who called it a publicity stunt.

It initially appeared that Potter had climbed the arch alone. The climber insisted his feat was ethical, as he left no traces of his climb on the famous rock. But video footage shot by two of his companions showed that at least one other man had scaled the arch with him. And photographs shot with a zoom lens later revealed three grooves worn by rope into the soft sandstone.

Potter insisted the rope marks were not his and apologized for upsetting others with his climb. "I climbed the arch in the highest and purest way I could, and I left it the same way I found it," he said in a statement. "But I failed to foresee how Delicate Arch for so many is also an untouchable symbol of our delicate relationship to nature."

If you're tempted to follow in Potter's footsteps, you may want to think again. At the time he made his notorious climb, scaling arches within the park was not explicitly forbidden. It is now.

To visit the arch enter Arches National Park ($10 per vehicle fee) and follow the signs to the Delicate Arch trailhead. The hike to the arch is moderately strenuous and takes about two hours round-trip. Bring lots of water and a camera. But you may want to leave your firewood and climbing ropes behind.

Watch for Falling Rock
Moab

The natural rock arch that appears on the Utah license plate, and lots of other places, is called Delicate Arch. But that's a misnomer. The real delicate arch is just a few miles away, also in Arches National Park, and it's called Landscape Arch. Maybe it just needs a better publicist.

An improbable ribbon of rock that stretches 306 feet—as long as a football field—from one cliff to another, Landscape Arch seems to defy gravity. Along with a similarly sized formation in Zion National Park, it's the longest natural-stone arch in the world. Park rangers say the most commonly asked question by tourists about the skinny arch is, "When's it gonna fall?"

Nobody knows, although geologists agree that erosion will collapse the arch eventually. In fact, it's already happening. In 1991 a 60-foot-long slab of sandstone broke off the underside of the arch and crashed to the desert below. Four years later a 30-foot-long piece fell.

No one was injured in either rock fall, although tourists, alerted by popping and cracking sounds coming from the arch, captured the 1995 episode on video. Rangers have closed the trail under the arch to prevent injuries to hikers.

So admire Landscape Arch while it still stands. And if you're beneath the arch and hear any snaps, crackles, and pops, run like crazy.

You'll find the arch in the north part of the park, along a 2-mile loop trail accessed from the Devil's Garden parking lot.

Would you stand under this? No? Good thinking.

Also in Moab:

The Slickrock Bike Trail, arguably the most famous mountain-biking trail in the world. This 12-mile loop, which attracts more than 100,000 fat-tire bikers annually, was actually developed in 1969 by motorcyclists.

The Apache Motel, where John Wayne, Henry Fonda, and others stayed while shooting Westerns nearby. The motel even features a John Wayne Suite. It's located at 166 South 400 East (435-259-5728).

The Moab Music Festival, which emphasizes classical chamber music, is held each year in late summer. The event's highlight is an outdoor concert in a natural red-rock grotto on the Colorado River, 30 miles downstream from Moab. Festival staffers use boats to ferry audience members, musicians, and their instruments—including a grand piano!—to the grotto and back. For more information visit www.moab musicfest.org.

Satan's Speedway
Monticello

It doesn't look too menacing in the daytime, but this 11-mile stretch of deserted Highway 491 from Monticello to the Colorado state line is one spooky road. You might even say it's possessed.

That's because until 2003 it was officially known as Route 666, or, more sardonically, the Devil's Highway, Satan's Speedway, or the Highway to Hell. According to legend, the road hosts several recurring apparitions: a pale girl in a white nightgown, a pack of demon dogs, a flaming high-speed truck, and a phantom car that appears during full moons and forces motorists off the two-lane road.

Route 666 took its name innocently enough in the 1950s as the sixth spur off Route 66, the fabled east-west highway of TV and song fame. It stretched from Monticello southeast to Gallup, New Mexico, a distance of 194 miles.

THE HOLE-IN-THE-ROCK EXPEDITION

Like those two dogs and the cat crossing miles of wilderness to find their way home, Utah has its own version of the *Incredible Journey*. It's called the Hole-in-the-Rock Expedition (no relation to the Hole n' the Rock cave home near Moab), and although there are no dogs or cats involved, it would also make a pretty good movie.

The story goes like this: Within several decades of the first Mormon pioneers' 1847 arrival in Salt Lake City, church members had colonized almost the entire region. The one area they hadn't settled, however, was the rugged country southeast of the Colorado River.

So in 1879 church leaders sought an expedition to cut a road into the unexplored region, opening it up for settlement. A hardy party of 250 men, women, and children volunteered for the arduous task. They had gathered that autumn at a spring south of Escalante to prepare for the journey when advance scouts returned to report that the area's rugged cliffs and mesas would make wagon travel almost impossible. By then, however, snow had blocked the pioneers' return to their former homes to the north. So, like a quarterback tossing a Hail Mary pass, they decided to try anyway.

With 80 wagons and 1,000 head of cattle, the party moved slowly across the rocky terrain. After two weeks, the explorers reached a seemingly insurmountable impasse: the 1,200-foot-deep Colorado River gorge. At the same time, they noticed a possible way down: a steep, narrow notch in the cliff.

Expedition members spent the next six weeks cutting and blasting away rock to create a tiny ribbon of road through the enlarged crevice, which they called the Hole in the Rock. They moved huge boulders and created a rough roadbed with logs, brush, and dirt, using wooden stakes to widen a narrow rock shelf. Then they used ropes to lower the wagons down the precarious slope—angled more than 25 degrees in places—to the river.

For some passengers, the descent was harrowing. One woman wrote, in a letter to her parents, "If you ever come this way it will scare you to death. It is about a mile from the top down to the river and it is almost straight down."

After navigating the Hole in the Rock, the party ferried across the Colorado and journeyed another 100 miles across deep ravines, up steep cliffs, and through thick cedar forests. Eventually they reached what is now Bluff, where they founded a settlement on the San Juan River that later spawned other towns in the region.

In total, the trek took six months. The pioneers depleted their food supplies and taxed themselves and their horses to exhaustion. Two babies were born during the journey; miraculously, nobody died. Those early explorers might be dismayed to learn that the route they established is now barely used, or that a car could make the same journey in half a day.

But the Hole-in-the-Rock Expedition stands more than a century later as a testament to pioneer grit and ingenuity. Coming soon to a theater near you?

Trail? I don't see no stinking trail!

But because 666 is cited as the "Number of the Beast" in modern texts of the Bible, some area residents grumbled that the digits could be seen as a Satanic symbol. Oliver Stone must have thought so, too—the highway is referenced in his 1994 movie, *Natural Born Killers*.

So New Mexico Gov. Bill Richardson responded to the complaints—not to mention the vandals who kept stealing the Highway 666 signs—by renaming the road. In a July 2003 ceremony, a Navajo medicine man blessed the newly christened highway to ward off any remaining evil spirits.

Some roadside merchants, who had sold "Highway 666" trinkets to tourists, objected to the name change. "They're making the devil mad," said one. So consider that the next time you drive the road. If you can help it, don't go at night. Don't drive the road under a full moon. And watch out for demon dogs.

The News of the Day—In A.D. 500
Monticello

It's called Newspaper Rock, but the headlines are hard to decipher. For that matter, so are the obituaries, the sports section, and the funny pages.

One of the largest and best-known Indian rock-art panels in Utah, Newspaper Rock is adorned with more than 300 figures and shapes, including deer, buffalo, a wheel with six spokes, and some stuff that's less easily identified, like the hulking creature with huge horns on top of its head. Or the bear-like footprint with six toes.

Ancestral Puebloan peoples probably carved the earliest shapes almost 2,000 years ago. More recently, Navajo and Ute Indians added their own figures to the tableau. Then there's the crudely scratched English-language graffiti, which I'm guessing has no anthropological significance whatsoever.

All the news that's fit to carve.

What do the figures mean? Most scholars believe they are ceremonial symbols or messages about hunting sites (i.e., "Littlefeather shot six deer here"). Because nobody knows for sure, we modern-day visitors are free to make up our own interpretations. Wedding announcements? Weather forecasts? An early form of Sudoku? The possibilities are endless.

Like an ancient Da Vinci Code, the Indian symbols of Newspaper Rock offer only tantalizing clues about their meanings. And that's what makes them cool.

To reach Newspaper Rock, head north from Monticello on Highway 191 and then head west on Highway 211. After 12 miles you'll see the large flat panel in a scenic, cottonwood-lined canyon. Across the road from the site are a primitive campground and a creek.

GEORGIE WHITE, WHITEWATER DAREDEVIL

Other river runners resented her brash antics. Raft passengers complained about her terrible food. But to many, she was a legend. Love her or hate her, one thing is clear: There will never be another Georgie White.

Born in Oklahoma in 1910, Georgie as a young woman joined up with a bicycle racing club who convinced her to come West. She was married twice, briefly, but domestic life didn't suit her—especially once White discovered river-running. "I fell in love with the river, married it, and I don't plan no divorce," she said.

In 1944, Georgie and a male friend decided to navigate the Colorado River through the Grand Canyon. There was only one problem: They couldn't afford a boat. So they swam down the river instead, buoyed by life preservers and surviving on dehydrated soup packed in watertight tins. They traveled 60 miles this way and had so much fun that they completed a longer "swim" down the canyon the next summer.

By 1951 the tough-talking Georgie had found herself an Army surplus neoprene raft, which she used to navigate the river on many solo trips. She then founded her River Rats rafting company, and with the help of volunteer boatmen (she preferred men) began taking passengers on commercial trips down the Colorado, Green, and San Juan Rivers.

Georgie was known for greeting boatmen at 5:00 a.m. by handing them a beer (on her trips she consumed little else). While other outfitters served fancy cuisine, she believed that river rafters should rough it. Breakfast was coffee and instant cereal. Lunch was a hard-boiled egg with taco sauce. Dinner, canned ravioli. On the last night of a trip, she'd mix all the leftovers in one pot and serve the result.

At the end of a successful trip Georgie initiated passengers into the Royal River Rats Society by breaking raw eggs over their heads. Her colorful ways drew the attention of the press. *Life* magazine called her an "iron-nerved mermaid." The *Los Angeles Times* profiled her at seventy-three as the "Grande Dame of the Grand Rapids" who wore a full-length leopard-skin leotard while holding the tiller in one hand and a beer in the other.Georgie White ran rivers until her death in 1992 at age eighty-one. Some people don't miss her.

Monumental Moves

Monument Valley

If you admire the stunning spires of stone rising abruptly from the desert floor in old Westerns like *Stagecoach and The Searchers,* don't thank John Ford or John Wayne. Thank Harry Goulding.

Harry and his wife, nicknamed "Mike," moved to remote Monument Valley in 1923 and opened a lodge and a trading post after gaining the trust of the local Navajos. In those days, Monument Valley was little known and accessible only by a dirt road.

Then came the Depression, which was hard on the Gouldings' business. So in 1938, when Harry Goulding heard that director John Ford was searching for a location to shoot a new Western, he got an idea. He loaded up his pickup truck, made the three-day drive to Los Angeles, and marched into Ford's studio office without an appointment.

Although Ford's secretary told him the director wasn't available, Harry was undeterred. He went out to his pickup, came back with a bedroll, and laid it on the office floor. When the secretary asked him what he was doing, Goulding said he planned to wait as long as it took for Ford to see him.

When the director eventually appeared, Harry showed him a stack of photos of Monument Valley, spreading them out on a bench. Ford and his location manager were so impressed that they decided shortly afterwards to shoot their movie, *Stagecoach*, there. Production started just two weeks later.

Ford went on to film seven of his most influential movies in Monument Valley, including 1956's *The Searchers*, considered by many the best Western ever made. His casts and crews stayed at Goulding's lodge during the shooting of each film. One film, *She Wore a Yellow Ribbon*, even shot scenes at the lodge.

These days Harry and Mike are gone. But Goulding's lodge, the only accommodations in Navajo-owned Monument Valley Tribal Park, is thriving. The modern-day complex includes a restaurant, pool, gift shop, and views of the valley's rock formations from each of its sixty rooms. It shows locally filmed Westerns nightly and offers guided tours of the valley's moviemaking locations.

Goulding's biggest curiosity, however, is the original 1920s trading post, which has been converted into a museum filled with historical artifacts and stills from movies shot nearby, from Ford's Westerns to Clint Eastwood's *The Eiger Sanction* to *Back to the Future, Part III*. The museum contains call sheets, a script for *Captain Buffalo*, and a guest book signed by John Wayne and Henry Fonda. Admission is $2.

Nearby is a small cabin that was used as Wayne's cavalry officer's quarters in *She Wore a Yellow Ribbon*. Inside a Wayne–like mannequin sits at a desk. It's not much of a likeness, but you get the idea.

Goulding's is located just west of Highway 163, yards north of the Arizona border. It's open year-round. For reservations call (435) 727-3231 or visit www.gouldings.com.

Run, Forrest, Run
Monument Valley

Monument Valley's best-known rock formations, the twin Mitten Buttes that you've see in the magazine and TV ads, lie several hundred yards south of the Utah border in Arizona. But many of the valley's other distinctive rocky spires are located just north in Utah. And they all have names.

There's the one that looks like a man sitting on a big chair ("King on His Throne"), the one that resembles hands clasped in prayer, or maybe an Indian headdress ("Big Indian"), the one that looks like a pair of animals ("Bear and Rabbit"), and the one that looks like an Old West stagecoach (called, amazingly enough, "Stagecoach").

These formations, spread in a line on a rough east-west axis, can be seen clearly from Highway 163 just north of the valley. In fact that stretch of road, which runs straight as an arrow across a barren desert plain towards the rocky buttes on the horizon, is one of the most photographed highways in the world.

Here's where Forrest Gump finally stopped running.

It's also where Tom Hanks, in the 1994 Best Picture–winner *Forrest Gump,* finally comes to his senses and quits running back and forth across the country. Remember the scene? Shaggy-haired Forrest, a pack of followers behind him, is jogging north on Highway 163 when he stops abruptly and turns around.

"Ah'm pretty tahhrd," he drawls. "Think I'll go home now." And with that he starts walking south, back towards the buttes, Alabama, and a haircut.

Thelma & Louise Ate Here

Thompson Springs

Thelma & Louise, the 1991 road movie starring Geena Davis and Susan Sarandon, has its footprints all over Utah.

The scene in which the fugitive women lock the police officer in the trunk of his car was shot in the Courthouse Towers section of Arches National Park. When Thelma and Louise drive off that cliff at the end? It's not the Grand Canyon but Dead Horse Point State Park on the Colorado River. And that nighttime scene when the two women stop for gas and use a diner pay phone to talk to Harvey Keitel, who tells them they're wanted for questioning and armed robbery? That was shot at the Silver Grill in this near-ghost town just north of I-70.

Like a lot of forgotten towns in the West, Thompson Springs sat along the once-popular Denver and Rio Grande Western Railroad line. In the early 1900s it had a hotel, a store, and a pool hall. With the demise of the railroad, however, the town all but died. The Silver Grill hung on for years but has now closed, too.

But it's forever immortalized on the silver screen.

UTAH'S AMELIA EARHART— IF SHE WERE A MAN, THAT IS

In November of 1934 a bold young vagabond named Everett Ruess led two burros into a remote Southern Utah gulch and vanished. He was only twenty-one. What happened to him? That question has haunted countless Western historians and writers—including Edward Abbey and Jon Krakauer—ever since. A young Kevin Costner wanted to play Ruess in a movie.

Some claim Ruess committed suicide. Others think he fell victim to anemia, or to cattle rustlers who mistook him for a detective. Still others believe he went to live with the Navajos or wandered south to Mexico. Most people, however, believe he drowned in the Colorado River or died in a fall.

Born in Hollywood, California, Ruess was an eccentric but affable fellow who during his brief life managed to befriend such famous Californians as photographer Ansel Adams. After discovering the Southwest on a trip to Navajo country when he was seventeen, Ruess devoted the last years of his life to wandering the desert. He documented his travels through journals and watercolor sketches, which only has added to his cult legend.

"I have not tired of the wilderness; rather I enjoy its beauty, and the vagrant life I lead, more keenly all the time," he wrote his brother. "I prefer the saddle to the streetcar and star-sprinkled sky to a roof . . . the deep peace of the wild to the discontent bred by cities."

Sheepherders last saw Ruess near Davis Gulch south of Escalante. After sharing their camp for two days, he packed up and set off. A search party found Ruess's burros, emaciated but alive, four months later. Neither he nor his gear were ever seen again.

The last clues to his whereabouts were a pair of inscriptions reading "Nemo 1934" on a rock not far from where he left the shepherds. Ruess was said to be an admirer of Jules Verne's classic *20,000 Leagues Under the Sea* and its adventurous Captain Nemo.

In a 1932 letter to his brother, Ruess seemed to foreshadow his mysterious fate. "I'll never stop wandering," he wrote. "And when the time comes to die, I'll find the wildest, loneliest, most desolate spot there is."

It appears he may have done just that.

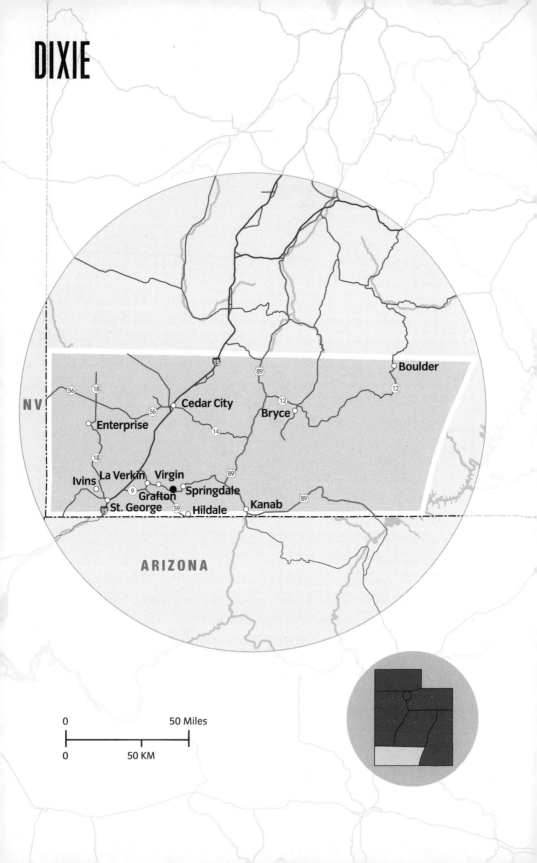

DIXIE

Boulder

NV

56
18
56
Cedar City
89
12
Bryce

Enterprise
14

18

Ivins
La Verkin
Virgin
9
Grafton
Springdale
89
St. George
59
Hildale
Kanab
89

ARIZONA

0   50 Miles

0   50 KM

DIXIE

The southwestern corner of Utah is called Dixie after its more famous Confederate namesake, and because Brigham Young sent settlers down here in the 1860s in an unsuccessful attempt to grow cotton. These days, however, the nickname applies more to the weather.

Compared to the rest of the state, it's pretty toasty down here.

Most of Utah lies on a high desert plateau some 4,300 to 6,000 feet above sea level. But south of Cedar City, the elevation dips below 3,000 feet, and the temperature rises accordingly. It's the only part of Utah where you'll see palm trees. No wonder Young made his winter home here, and why retirees have made St. George the fastest-growing part of the state.

Maybe the heat makes some folks in Dixie a little nutty. How else can we explain a town that declares itself a "United Nations–free zone," a museum filled with hundreds of stuffed wild animals shot by the curator himself, an outdoor theater where a flash flood washes across the stage, and the nation's largest sanctuary for homeless pets, where pooches live together in a compound called Dogtown?

Nearby is Kanab, Utah's golden-age movie capital, where you can visit sets from Clint Eastwood Westerns and sleep in the same motel room that Ronald Reagan did a half-century ago.

I wish I was in Dixie, Hooray! Hooray!

And I haven't even mentioned what may be the strangest part of Dixie culture: plural marriage, still alive and well. Hildale, along with its sister town across the Arizona border, is home to some 10,000 modern-day polygamists—the largest such group in the country. It's not a tourist town, exactly, but you can drive through for a glimpse of something truly curious.

To Hell's Backbone and Back
Boulder

Hey, you thrill-seekers, do we have a white-knuckle drive for you: It's called Hell's Backbone Road, and it's probably not on your AAA atlas. Local maps show it as a 44-mile loop off Highway 12 that winds through the Dixie National Forest between Boulder and Escalante. Satan, if he's ever around, would probably describe it differently.

An impressive feat of engineering, the gravel byway seems tame enough at first as it switchbacks up a mountain. But there's a 12-mile stretch in the middle where the road crosses a narrow alpine ridge with steep drop-offs on both sides.

Here the margin for error grows slim. There are no guardrails, no shoulders, and drops of almost 2,000 feet out each window. Two cars approaching each other have to proceed *very* slowly. The road also crosses a single-lane bridge over a deep gorge with the cheery name of Death Hollow Canyon.

Alrighty then! Pile into the car, kids!

One motorist, in a firsthand account on the Internet, says he's driven almost every posted road between the Sierras and the Rockies, "and nothing has come close to this backway for sheer exhilaration."

By "exhilaration," I think he means, "terror."

If you're still game, you can access the byway (also known by the more benign name of Posey Lake Road) 3 miles west of Boulder on Highway 12. Allow about two hours for the trip. High-clearance vehicles are recommended, and the road is closed in winter.

Noah's Ark, Stuffed into a Museum
Bryce

Robert Driedonks loves wild animals. He also loves to hunt. So he channeled his two passions into creating a museum containing more than 600 species of taxidermied critters, most of which he shot himself. The result is the Paunsaugunt Wildlife Museum, a unique tribute to one man's unusual dream.

"My whole life is in there," says Robert of his exotic attraction near the entrance to Bryce Canyon National Park. "I hunt them all myself. It's been a little tough—it's cost me quite a few wives, trust me."

Driedonks says he became obsessed with wild animals as a boy growing up in rugged British Columbia. By the age of 16 he dreamed of opening his own wildlife museum to share his hobby with the world. Over the next three decades, he traveled to Africa, Australia, Europe, Alaska, and around the continental United States, hunting exotic animals and having them stuffed. He also has educational permits allowing him to gather animals that have died naturally in the wild.

By the mid-1990s, Robert had finally collected enough specimens, and money, to open his Paunsaugunt museum in nearby Panguitch. In 2006 he moved the 14,000-square-foot museum—named for a Paiute Indian term—to its current home. The building contains dozens of dioramas, augmented by detailed murals, showcasing everything from lions, tigers, and giraffes to birds, bears, bobcats, and beavers.

"Everything is in its natural habitat," he says of his taxidermy collection, worth more than $2 million. "There's no glass in front of the scenes, so you don't feel like you're looking into a box."

Among the exhibits is a display of stuffed sea creatures, most of which Robert hooked himself, plus row after row of wall-mounted heads of antelope, deer, elk, zebras, and other huntable species. Also on view are collections of 600 seashells, almost 1,000 insects, and some 1,400 butterflies. Not all the animals are dead; across the road is an elk preserve, also owned by Robert, where visitors can take wagon rides past the herds.

Stuffed animals galore – many of them shot by the owner – fill the Paunsaugunt Wildlife Museum.

Despite its size, the new museum still isn't big enough to hold Robert's growing collection. He's got 80 stuffed animals in storage, plus another 150 left to him by a taxidermist pal who died recently. But at least he's no longer collecting wives. Fourth and current wife Teri understands his wildlife obsessions and even goes hunting with him.

The Paunsaugunt Wildlife Museum is open April 1 through November 1. For more info call (435) 834-5555 (summer) or (702) 877-2664 (winter); or visit www.brycecanyonwildlifemuseum.com.

The Horse That Founded a University
Cedar City

Bronzed horses usually are afterthoughts—anonymous props for the heroes sitting atop them. But a dramatic statue on the campus of Southern Utah University, which depicts a gallant horse straining to pull a sleigh through deep snow, is not a tribute to the men behind him clutching his reins. It's a tribute to the horse.

When the college was founded in 1897, it held classes in Cedar City's social hall. But that fall Utah's new attorney general ruled that the college would have to move elsewhere unless the city built proper academic buildings—one building, even—by the next school year.

The townspeople donated their time and money to tackle the building. But city leaders, facing a tight deadline, were in a bind. They'd used up all their available lumber to build the social hall. There was plenty of timber in the mountains to the east, but it was winter and the heavy snows made travel almost impossible.

On January 5, 1898, a group of men journeyed into the mountains to cut the trees needed to erect the building. The snow was waist deep, obliterating the trail. The men were in danger of being trapped in the mountains when they put an unnamed sorrel horse at the front of their procession.

The chestnut-colored horse, nicknamed Old Sorrel, waded tirelessly into the drifts over and over until they gave way. He'd pause, sit back on his haunches, heave a big sigh, and then start again. Thanks to Old Sorrel, the maiden party returned to Cedar City alive.

Emboldened by this success, city fathers made repeated trips into the mountains to gather wood. The college's building was completed that fall, and the school would eventually become a modern state university, home today to more than 7,000 students.

Nobody seems to know what became of the horse or where he is buried. But that original building, called Old Main, still stands on campus. And so does Old Sorrel, immortalized in bronze.

BABY, BABY, BABY

If you notice kids almost everywhere you look in Utah, you're not imagining things. Utah has the highest birth rate in the nation—an average of two-and-a-half children per woman, which is half a child higher than the national rate.

Most people attribute this to the Mormon Church's emphasis on large families; it's not unusual in Utah to see parents with seven or eight children. The high birthrate manifests itself in lots of schools, lots of minivans, and lots of family-oriented entertainment, from musicals to Disney movies to Disney movie musicals such as the popular *High School Musical* and its sequel.

Those movies were filmed in—you guessed it!—Utah.

DIXIE

Brush Up on Your Shakespeare
Cedar City

When the British Broadcasting Company went looking in 1981 for a replica of an Elizabethan–era theater in which to film part of a series on William Shakespeare, they turned to, of all places, this remote college town.

Boy, they sure must have been desperate, right? Well, not exactly. Turns out that the Adams Shakespearean Theatre, built in 1977 on the campus of Southern Utah University, is a strikingly authentic reproduction of the open-air playhouses, such as the original Globe, popular with Londoners in the Bard's day.

The play's the thing at this authentic Shakespearean stage in Cedar City.

The 819-seat theatre, patterned after drawings of 16th-century Tudor stages, is the focal point of the Utah Shakespearean Festival, which mounts nine plays every June through October. Founded in 1961 by Fred C. Adams, a young New York actor who came west to teach drama at what was then called the College of Southern Utah, the festival has grown from a grass-roots, all-volunteer enterprise into one of the finest Shakespeare theater companies in the nation. In 2000 the festival even won a Tony.

The outdoor Adams theatre—named not for Fred but an early supporter of the festival—still plays host to Shakespeare plays each summer. Beside the theatre is a shady courtyard that comes alive each summer evening with costumed barkers, minstrels, and drama students with fake British accents selling meat pasties—a taste of Merry Olde England in a place you'd never expect it.

The Utah Shakespearean Festival is headquartered at 351 West Center Street. For more information and a schedule of plays, visit www.bard.org.

Also in Cedar City:

The Iron Mission State Park Museum, which contains pioneer and Indian artifacts and a Butch Cassidy–era stagecoach riddled with bullet holes. It's located at 635 North Main Street (435-586-9290).

The Other September 11
Enterprise

On September 11, 1857, in a grassy valley some 10 miles southeast of this town, occurred one of the darkest episodes in American history. It's known today as the Mountain Meadows Massacre, and it was believed to be the largest mass slaughter of civilians on U.S. soil until the 1995 Oklahoma City bombing.

This rock mound memorializes the victims of the Mountain Meadows Massacre.

The victims were members of a Western-bound group of Arkansas pioneers led by Alexander Fancher. The Fancher party, as they became known, reached Utah at a time when tensions between the Mormon-run territory and the U.S. government were on the verge of boiling over. Brigham Young had declared martial law, and U.S. Army troops were advancing on Salt Lake City, creating a climate that was hostile to outsiders.

The Fancher party had reached Mountain Meadows, a well-known stopover on the Old Spanish Trail, when they were attacked by a group of Paiute Indians and Mormon militiamen dressed as Native Americans. After a five-day siege, the wagon train was approached by militia officer John D. Lee, who said he had negotiated a truce with the Paiutes and arranged for the pioneers to be escorted safely to Cedar City.

The Fancher party members accepted, but shortly after they left their encircled wagons they were massacred by Paiutes and militiamen hidden nearby. Estimates of those killed range from 82 to 120. Although those involved swore each other to secrecy, word leaked out and Lee was eventually executed for his role in the massacre.

No, it's not a cheery story. It's also a highly sensitive and controversial one, especially within Mormon circles. Outside of Utah, however, it's remarkable how few people know about it. That may change with the 2007 release of *September Dawn,* a movie about the massacre starring Jon Voight as Lee.

Several outdoor memorials just off Highway 18 commemorate the massacre site. A 200-yard paved path leads to a granite memorial on a hill overlooking the meadow. Nearby, a mile-long gravel road leads into the meadow and another memorial in the shape of a burial mound.

Butch and Sundance's Playground
Grafton

Remember that scene early in *Butch Cassidy and the Sundance Kid* when Paul Newman and Katharine Ross ride a bicycle around a yard to the tune of "Raindrops Keep Falling On My Head"? Even though it's not raining?

Well, the whole thing was filmed in Grafton, a pioneer village-turned-ghost-town in the shadow of the towering cliffs of Zion National Park. Founded in 1859 by Mormon settlers, Grafton was nearly wiped out several times by flooding from the Virgin River. But pioneers persevered, and the town was bustling until shortly after the turn of the 20th century, when a canal was dug to nearby Hurricane and most townspeople left for better pastures. The rare ghost town that died before electricity came, Grafton sat almost empty until 1944, when the last couple left.

In recent years, a group of preservationists have begun restoring Grafton's historic buildings, starting with the town's 1886 one-room schoolhouse. The handsome adobe structure with its simple bell tower, framed against dramatic red-rock cliffs, has become one of the most photographed ghost-town buildings in the American West.

Now the heritage group is restoring Grafton's five remaining wood-frame homes to preserve the town as a historic site. Visitors will find the houses in various stages of restoration, plus a town cemetery, half a mile to the south, with some seventy-five graves. The weathered headstones include the graves of three brothers who were killed by Indians on the same day in 1866.

Robert Redford liked the town so much he returned here eleven years after *Butch & Sundance* to film scenes for his Jane Fonda romance, *The Electric Horseman*. To visit Grafton go just west of Rockville on Highway 9 and turn south at the sign. A winding dirt road leads to the town. Or for more information visit www.graftonheritage.org.

The, Um, Polygamy Capital of the Nation

Hildale

The Church of Jesus Christ of Latter-day Saints, as Mormons are officially known, outlawed polygamy in 1890. But a splinter group of religious fundamentalists have been practicing plural marriage, mostly
quietly, for decades in this town on the Utah-Arizona state line. Hildale
and its sister town across the border, Colorado City, are home to some
10,000 polygamists—the largest such community in the United States.

The group, which split from the Mormon Church more than a century ago, is known as the Fundamentalist Church of Jesus Christ of Latter-day Saints, or FLDS for short. It chose the desert border location in
1928 for its remoteness and for the hassles authorities would
encounter in trying to prosecute them in two states. Church members
are expected to contribute their income to a United Effort Plan that
holds in trust private property, including most of the towns' houses.

Tourists can drive through Hildale, although it's not an especially
hospitable place. FLDS followers are mistrustful of outsiders, so be pre-
pared for some strange looks. FLDS church leaders preach unquestion-
ing obedience, instruct townspeople to avoid TV, and urge them to
prepare for an impending apocalypse that will wipe out all but the most
devout.

The town's houses, most of them built in the last few decades, are
enormous to accommodate multiple wives plus children. Many homes
appear unfinished, however, and lawns or landscaping is almost nonex-
istent. Most women in town wear ankle-length pioneer dresses, and,
after a recent church edict banning recreational activities, few children
play in the streets. NO TRESPASSING signs are everywhere.

The twin towns were once known as Short Creek. They made
national headlines in 1953 when Arizona authorities descended upon
the towns, arrested 31 men for practicing polygamy, and took 263

women and children into temporary custody. But the raid backfired, winning public sympathy for the polygamists and costing the Arizona governor his re-election.

The towns were left in peace for almost fifty years, although they did appear in a 1981 Hollywood movie, *The Child Bride of Short Creek*, starring a young Diane Lane. A photograph of the towns also graced the cover of Jon Krakauer's 2003 best seller, *Under the Banner of Heaven*, which chronicled the sometimes-violent history of Mormon extremism.

In recent years Utah authorities have cracked down on what they describe as a troubling pattern of underage FLDS girls being forced into marriages with much older men. Eight men in the community have been charged with various sex crimes for their alleged marriages to young girls.

FLDS president Warren Jeffs, whom the community considers a prophet, is estimated to have forty wives and more than fifty children. Jeffs went into hiding in 2005 after he was charged with arranging marriages between men and underage girls. He was on the FBI's 10 Most Wanted list when arrested in August 2006 in Las Vegas, throwing the future of the FLDS community into question.

Now Playing Nightly: Live Animals and a Flash Flood
Ivins

Nothing enlivens a theatrical show like 60,000 gallons of water washing across the stage. But they've pulled that unlikely feat off nightly at the Tuacahn Center for the Performing Arts, an outdoor theater framed by a towering red-rock canyon that's one of the most unusual theatrical backdrops you'll ever see.

The $23 million Tuacahn complex opened in 1995 with an indoor theater, a dance studio, a recital hall, and a performing-arts high school. The sandstone brick in its plaza came from the same quarry in India that produced the Taj Mahal. But the jewel of the place, founded by Utah playwright Doug Stewart, is its 1,920-seat outdoor venue, which is encircled by 1,500-foot high cliffs.

Tuacahn's opening show, *UTAH!,* told the historical saga of Jacob Hamblin, a Mormon pioneer who defied 19th-century history by making a treaty with Southern Utah's Indians and then honoring it. *UTAH!* was staged nightly with a massive cast, live horses, blazing wagons, fireworks, and—in what became the highlight of the evening—a flash flood designed to reenact an actual 1862 flood that lasted forty days. Hidden pipes pumped a torrent of water across the specially designed stage and into storm drains.

UTAH! ran for four summers—no, nobody drowned—before Tuacahn's creative team replaced it with Broadway musicals. But they didn't completely retire the flood, bringing it back for added drama in *Seven Brides for Seven Brothers* and *Fiddler on the Roof.* In 2004 the flood returned for a tailor-made appearance in—what else?—*Singing in the Rain.*

Ironically, a real flash flood engulfed the complex several months after it opened in 1995, filling the school's interior with knee-high mud. Maybe Mother Nature was angry at not being cast.

For more information about Tuacahn or for tickets, call (435) 652-3300 or visit www.tuacahn.org.

YOU SAY DESERT, I SAY DESERET

If you spend any time in Utah, you'll notice the word "Deseret" everywhere. As in Deseret Book stores, the Deseret Credit Union and the *Deseret Morning News* newspaper.

What's wrong with these people, you might ask? They live in a desert but they can't spell it?

Deseret is actually a Book of Mormon term meaning "honeybee," which explains why Utah's official nickname is the Beehive State instead of, say, the Osmond State. When Mormon pioneers settled the area in 1847, they called their provisional state Deseret and even petitioned Congress for statehood under that name. The borders of the proposed state brashly included what is now western Colorado, most of Arizona and almost all of present-day Nevada.

But the U.S. government never recognized the name, and national anti-Mormon sentiment at the time eventually doomed the fledgling state's moniker. In 1850 Congress created the Utah Territory in recognition of the Ute Indians who called the area home.

The territory's borders were shrunk, too. Maybe that's just as well. Can you imagine "Las Vegas, Utah?" Me, neither.

Is This Pet Heaven? No, It's Utah

Kanab

If you're an orphaned dog or cat, you could do a lot worse than end up at the Best Friends Animal Sanctuary. You'll get a healthy diet of food, veterinary care, room to rest or run around, and plenty of furry pals to play with. And unlike the pound, you can stay here as long as you want without fear of being, um, terminated.

Located on a 33,000-acre ranch 5 miles north of Kanab—in a canyon where Hollywood once filmed Westerns—Best Friends is the nation's largest sanctuary for homeless animals. On any given day the place is home to about 1,500 dogs, cats, horses, rabbits, goats, birds, and other critters—shipped in from around the country and sometimes even overseas.

In 2004 a team from the sanctuary rescued some 4,000 dogs and cats from the floodwaters of New Orleans following Hurricane Katrina. In 2006 Best Friends airlifted 300 cats and dogs to Utah from war-torn Lebanon. These efforts are funded by dues from 300,000 Best Friends members nationwide, 90 percent of them women, plus donations from other animal lovers.

About three of every four animals arriving at Best Friends are soon placed with adoptive families in good homes. Others who are old, crippled, or too traumatized from mistreatment to be adopted find permanent homes at Best Friends. Except in cases of terminal and painful illness, animals at Best Friends are never destroyed, no matter how crowded the sanctuary gets.

Tourists are welcome to come visit the animals. The sanctuary offers ninety-minute tours of its facility every day, with stops at each of the segregated, and cutely named, animal compounds: Dogtown, Cat World, Horse Haven, and the Bunny House. The tour also stops at the sanctuary's two bird compounds: Feathered Friends (for domesticated

Both the pets and the people are happy at Best Friends Animal Sanctuary.

birds like parakeets) and Wild Friends, for hawks, owls, and other untamed birds.

Best Friends also has an animal cemetery with hundreds of tiny headstones—including a memorial for the thousands of pets lost in Hurricane Katrina.

Visitors can volunteer to help work with the animals and can even adopt them. Best Friends also offers "sleepovers"—trial overnight stays with prospective adoptee pets so that owners can make sure they click with the animal. A puppy—how's that for a memorable Utah souvenir?

For more information about the sanctuary and its programs, visit www.bestfriends.org.

They Did the Hokey Pokey in the Moqui

Kanab

You won't find stalagmites or stalactites in Moqui Cave, a roadside attraction 6 miles north of Kanab on Highway 89. But you will find a unique museum with a colorful history. You see, Moqui Cave used to be a dance hall.

Let's start from the beginning. The cave's legacy as a drinkers' hideout dates back to Prohibition, when folks held illicit parties in its sloping, 200-foot depths. In 1951 a colorful lapsed Mormon and ex-pro football player named Garth Chamberlain bought the place and decided to turn it into a tavern.

Garth and his wife Laura cleaned out the beer bottles and scrubbed the graffiti off the walls. Then they leveled the floor with 150 truckloads of dirt, covered it with 7,000 square feet of concrete, painted the walls white, and built a stage for the orchestra. Garth, who was something of a rockhound, also installed a bar inlaid with a mosaic of colored stones.

The place was a popular watering hole for a while, especially among the workers in the 1960s who built nearby Glen Canyon Dam.

By the late 1970s, however, Garth had wearied of the party life. He closed the bar and turned the cave into a museum to display all the rocks, fossils, and other artifacts he'd collected over the years. When he died of a heart attack, his son Lex took over management of the place.

Today Lex and his wife Lee Anne run the Moqui (pronounced "MO-kee") Cave with seasonal help from their five kids. The former dance floor now houses a display of more than 140 varieties of fluorescent rocks, which glow in the dark under invisible ultraviolet light. Another room of the cave holds a gift shop and some 180 fossilized dinosaur tracks. And the former bar area now showcases centuries-old Native American sandals, pottery, and a collection of 3,000 arrowheads.

Best of all: The natural temperature inside the cave holds steady at or near a pleasant 70 degrees year-round—even during the scorching southern Utah summers, when 100-degree days are common. Admission is $4 for adults, and the cave is open all year. For more info call (435) 644-8525 or visit www.moquicave.com.

BET YOU DIDN'T KNOW THEY WERE FROM UTAH

Pretty much everyone knows that the Osmonds are from Utah and that NBA legend Karl Malone isn't. But did you know about these other famous Beehive Staters?

Maude Adams. Born in 1872 in Salt Lake City, the stage actress became known in theaters around the country, especially for her signature role as Peter Pan in J.M. Barrie's children's classic. Jane Seymour's character in the 1980 film romance *Somewhere in Time* was based on her.

Roseanne Barr. The "domestic goddess" and TV star was born in Salt Lake City in 1952 to working-class Jewish-Mormon parents. Before making it big as a comedienne she washed dishes in a Salt Lake restaurant.

Wilford Brimley. This Utah rancher-turned-actor's name may not ring a bell right away, but his face sure will. His gruff, mustachioed presence enlivened such movies as *The Natural, Cocoon,* and *The Firm,* although he may be best known for the TV commercials he made for Quaker Oats.

Nolan K. Bushnell. The Clearfield native is considered by many the father of the video-game industry. He co-founded the Atari Corp. and helped create Pong, the world's first popular video game.

Ben Cook, text-messaging champ. As a Provo teenager, Cook set a Guinness world record in 2004 by text-messaging the phrase, "The razor-toothed piranhas of the genera *Serrasalmus* and *Pygocentrus* are the most ferocious freshwater fish in the world. In reality, they seldom attack a human," in fifty-seven seconds. Two years later, Cook's nimble fingers set a new record when he texted the same phrase in forty-two seconds.

Mrs. Fields. Cookie queen Debbi Fields launched her empire in 1977 from Park City, where she was born.

Gene Fulmer. The West Jordan native and dogged middleweight boxing champion was known for his epic 1950s bouts with Sugar Ray Robinson.

Anthony Geary. Born in the little mountain town of Coalville, Geary found fame in the 1970s and 1980s on *General Hospital* as curly-haired Luke Spencer, a character some consider the most popular in soap-opera history. Remember "Luke and Laura?" I thought so.

Ken Jennings. This former Murray software engineer won a record seventy-four consecutive games and $2.5 million on *Jeopardy!* in 2004 before finally losing on a question about tax-preparation firm H&R Block.

J. Willard Marriott. Raised on a farm near Ogden, he parlayed a Washington, D.C., root beer stand into an international hotel chain.

Merlin Olsen. This bearded NFL Hall of Famer, who later starred on TV in *Father Murphy* and in ads for FTD florists, was born in Logan in 1940.

Evelyn Wood. The speed-reading queen, who could digest a reported 2,700 words per minute, was born in Logan.

Fay Wray. Before finding worldwide fame with a big ape in the original *King Kong,* the Canadian-born actress lived with her Mormon parents in Salt Lake City.

Loretta Young. Born in Salt Lake City in 1913, the actress won an Oscar in 1947 for her performance in *The Farmer's Daughter* and later hosted the long-running *Loretta Young Show* on TV. Her 1935 affair with Clark Gable caused a stir after she became pregnant and took a "vacation" to have the baby in secret.

Dinner and a Movie Set

Kanab

Part restaurant, part museum, part hokey tourist attraction, Frontier Movie Town is a must for any fan of old-time Westerns. Their slogan: "Where the West is Fun!" And they have a point: Where else can you eat barbecue while scoping out rustic wooden sets from *The Outlaw Josey Wales?*

The front of the place is a kitschy Wild West street, with sculptures of cowboys on bucking broncos and a wall where tourists can poke their faces through holes to be photographed as gunslingers, frontier gals, and so on. Inside, the restaurant's walls are filled with movie posters and signed photos of old-time stars. Some of the autographs, like Jimmy Stewart's, are clearly forged.

But the real draws are the old movie sets on the back lot, near the outdoor bar, barbecue grill, and patio. Salvaged from sites in and around Kanab where the movies were actually filmed, the rickety sets and props include a gun port from *Sergeants 3,* a Rat Pack Western starring Dean Martin and Frank Sinatra; an old windmill from *Truth or Consequences, N.M.,* a 1997 Kiefer Sutherland crime caper; a bench from the *F-Troop* TV series, and even a set from an 1980s Kenny Loggins video.

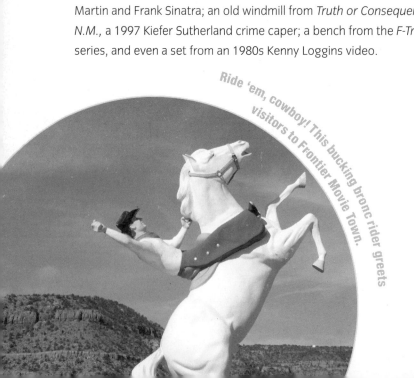

Ride 'em, cowboy! This bucking bronc rider greets visitors to Frontier Movie Town.

Best represented, however, is *The Outlaw Josey Wales*, the 1976 Clint Eastwood Western about a farmer seeking vengeance on the soldiers who killed his family. Here you'll find an adobe ranch house (actually made from fiberglass) and stables used in the movie, which was mostly shot around Kanab and Lake Powell. The feel of the place is authentic enough that you can almost see squinty-eyed Clint emerge through the dust, pistols blazing.

Frontier Movie Town is located at 297 West Center Street. Admission is free. For more information call (800) 551-1714.

Visitors to Frontier Movie Town will see old sets from *The Outlaw Josey Wales*.

Ronald Reagan Slept Here
Kanab

Step into the lobby of the Parry Lodge and you're greeted by dozens of familiar faces, staring back at you from framed photos on the walls: Frank Sinatra, Jane Russell, James Garner, Tony Curtis, John Wayne. All of them stayed at the hotel in the 1930s through the 1960s, when Kanab was called "Little Hollywood" because of all the Westerns shot there.

Ronald Reagan and Frank Sinatra are among the movie stars who stayed at this Kanab hotel back in the day.

The three Parry brothers—Whit, Gron, and Chance—opened the hotel in 1931, the year after Wayne filmed his first movie nearby. Envisioning his lodge as a potential base for movie crews, Whit Parry brought photographs of the desert scenery to Hollywood, hoping to lure filmmakers. It worked: Over the next forty years more than a hundred movies and TV shows were shot at least partly in the area.

With its swimming pool and elegant dining room, the Parry became a home away from home for movie stars, most of them represented in the lobby. Tim Conway, ever the jokester, signed his photo, "We'll always be in touch—because I'm not paying my bill."

Of course, Hollywood doesn't make many Westerns anymore, and Parry Lodge's heyday as a celebrity crash pad is long gone. But its aura of fading glamor still remains: It's hard not to be impressed by the row of original motel–style rooms with the names of their famous former occupants painted above the doors: Dean Martin. Tyrone Power. Gregory Peck. That Sinatra fellow. And yes, a pre-White House Ronald Reagan.

Behind the main lodge is an old barn that hosts nightly screenings of movies, such as *The Desperadoes*, that were filmed in Kanab. The barn was once used to stable horses used in the films, including Roy Rogers's Trigger and the Lone Ranger's Silver.

The Parry Lodge is open year-round at 89 East Center Street. For reservations call (800) 748-4104.

Gunsmoke's Ghosts

Kanab

East of Kanab in a picturesque canyon is a weathered Wild West set where they shot movies, TV shows, commercials, and countless bad guys. It's the Johnson Canyon Movie Set, and it's one of the few remaining historic on-location sets in the West.

The Johnson Canyon set hasn't been used onscreen in more than two decades, and its buildings look like they'd collapse under a stiff wind. But in its 1950s and 1960s heyday, it swarmed with gunslingers, gamblers, barmaids, sheriffs, and outlaws. Charlton Heston and Rhonda Fleming kissed on the dance hall steps in *Pony Express*.

The set was home to the *Death Valley Days* TV series and such movies as Frank Capra's *Westward the Women,* and *MacKenna's Gold* with Gregory Peck and Omar Sharif. The long-running TV Western *Gunsmoke* filmed here in 1955 before moving to sets in Southern California.

Some episodes of *Gunsmoke* were shot here.

Still standing along a north-south axis are a dozen or so rickety wooden buildings, including a barn, a saloon, several other storefronts, and a gallows. The set is closed to the public, although the owners of the property hope to restore it as a tourist attraction. To get a look at the set head east from Kanab 10 miles, then turn north into Johnson Canyon and go 5 miles. The set will be on your right, clearly visible from the road.

Also in Kanab:

Denny's Wigwam, perhaps southern Utah's largest retailer of Old West and Indian clothes, jewelry, rugs, saddles, and collectibles. Customers can pose for photos in a stagecoach out front. You'll find it at 78 East Center Street (435-644-2452).

United against the U.N.
La Verkin

This town of 3,400 people west of Zion National Park looks quiet enough. But folks here are an especially independent-minded, feisty bunch—especially when it comes to international politics.

In 2001 La Verkin became the first municipality in the nation to declare itself a United Nations–free zone. The ordinance, passed 3-2 by the city council on July 4 no less, prohibited use of the U.N. insignia on city property and the expenditure of any city funds on the global organization.

City leaders pushed the law as a show of protest, arguing that the United Nations should not direct U.S. foreign policy. Under the ordinance, La Verkin residents who backed the U.N. could still do so as long as they filed an annual report with the city.

But while La Verkin is a conservative town, some of its residents thought the measure was, well, a little silly. "This is dumb," said one woman. "Why is it any of their business to deal with the United Nations? They should fix the potholes."

Perhaps embarrassed by the mocking international headlines, the La Verkin council repealed the ordinance in 2003. The law's chief backer gathered enough signatures to get the measure on the November election ballot that year, where it was defeated 427 to 321.

So Kofi Annan and the U.N.'s General Assembly are once again free to visit La Verkin anytime. I'm sure they're making their vacation plans now.

MOLLIE'S NIPPLES

For some reason Utah has at least five, and possibly as many as seven, pointy peaks named Mollie's Nipple or Molly's Nipple. There's one in the northeast part of the state, one in the west desert, one southeast of Provo, and one in the hills above Hurricane, east of St. George.

Who was Mollie, and why did everyone seem to know what her nipples looked like? Pioneer history isn't clear on this, although a book called *Utah Place Names* offers a clue. According to the book, the tallest of the Mollie's Nipples, at 7,271 feet, is in Kane County. Local cowhands say the peak was "named as a compliment" to Mollie Kitchen, wife of pioneer settler John Kitchen, who owned a ranch nearby.

Named by her husband, I presume.

Seven Rooms for Seven Wives

St. George

As you might guess, the Seven Wives Inn has a polygamist history. This handsome B&B was built in 1873 by Mormon pioneer Edwin G. Woolley, who, after the United States outlawed polygamy in 1882, hid some polygamist friends for a time in his attic, which was accessed only by a secret door.

At the Seven Wives Inn, you can soak inside a 1927 Model T Ford.

One of these polygamists was Benjamin F. Johnson, who really did have seven wives. The inn today is run by one of Johnson's descendants, Brent Calder, and his wife, Vanessa.

The inn is split into three buildings: the original Woolley home, a cottage out back, and the "president's house" next door, which hosted some of the early presidents of the LDS Church. The main house has seven bedrooms, each one named for a different plural wife: the Harriett room, the Lucinda room, and so on.

The hidden attic, now the Jane room, can be yours for $95 a night. For a $185-a-night splurge, try the Sarah Suite, which has two fireplaces and a bathroom Jacuzzi tub built into a 1927 Ford Model T.

The Seven Wives Inn is located at 217 North 100 West. For more history or maybe a reservation, call (800) 600-3737 or visit www.seven wivesinn.com.

Also in St. George:

The St. George Dinosaur Discovery Site, which has a large collection of fossilized dinosaur tracks. It's located at 2180 East Riverside Drive (435-574-DINO).

The Blue Bunny, an enormous ice-cream parlor with towering ice-cream cone sculptures, an interactive light show, and singing and dancing servers. You'll find it at 20 North Main Street (435-674-9393).

Where Angels Don't Fear to Tread—But You Might

Springdale

Want to test your physical and psychological limits? You can spend a day in a sweatlodge, go bungee jumping, or join the Marines. Or you can just climb Angels Landing, in Zion National Park.

One of the most exhilarating hikes in the national park system, the trail is not for the faint of heart. Starting from the floor of Zion Canyon, it ascends 1,488 feet to a lofty perch atop a towering monolith of rock. But that's just part of the story.

The hike got its name in 1916 when explorer Frederick Fisher gazed up at the spire and said, "Only an angel could land on it." By the time Zion became a national park in 1919, climbers were determined to prove him wrong.

Hikers navigate Walter's Wiggles inside Zion National Park.

Climb this, if you dare.

The trail starts out tamely enough as it ascends a series of looping switchbacks that hug the side of the canyon wall. After about a mile, the path plunges into a shady, tree-lined ravine called Refrigerator Canyon because the temperature there is always cooler than the more exposed trail.

Refrigerator Canyon ends at a series of twenty-one sharp man-made switchbacks, nicknamed Walter's Wiggles for Walter Ruesch, the first superintendent of Zion, who helped build them. This crowd-pleasing part of trail inspires jokes by hikers about how it's time to "squiggle the wiggles."

The wiggles lead to a flat sandy lookout with a great view. But the scary part is just beginning. The last segment of the trail winds up a narrow sandstone ridge with sheer, thousand-foot drop-offs on either side. Chains are anchored to the rock to offer grips. Even so, it's not uncommon to encounter hikers along this stretch who are paralyzed with fear and unable to go on.

The trail culminates on a plateau with a stunning, panoramic view of Zion Canyon. Here you can rest, drink some water, and congratulate yourself for making it to the top.

To access the Angels Landing trailhead, take the Zion Canyon shuttle bus to the Grotto stop and follow the signs. Mortals make the round-trip hike in four to five hours. Angels do it a little faster.

For more info visit www.utah.com/nationalparks/zion/angels_landing.

Also in Springdale:

The Zion Canyon Elk Ranch, where visitors can gaze at an assortment of elk, buffalo, longhorn cattle, and miniature donkeys. Tourists can buy feed pellets and feed the animals. Some of the elk are so tame they'll eat from your hand. You'll find the ranch on the main drag in the center of town.

If Roger Rabbit Was a Cowboy, He'd Live Here

Virgin

Nobody can say Andy and Denise Anderson don't have a sense of humor. The couple owns the Fort Zion Virgin Trading Post, a peculiar tourist stop along the road to Zion National Park. What's peculiar about it? Well, for starters, it has the Virgin Village, a cartoonish Wild West town complete with stylized, Looney Tune–like creations of a bank, a jail, and a saloon.

If you're looking for a kitschy Western photo op, here's your place.

Behind the cartoon town is a Western-themed petting zoo (admission $1). It houses a pony named Butch, a donkey named Sundance, a llama nicknamed Jesse James, and a menagerie of tame deer, lambs, ferrets, and bighorn sheep.

Inside, the gift shop sells ice cream with such exotic flavors as Cactus Coconut (made from real prickly-pear cactus), Very Rocky Road, and something called Dirt and Worms. The gift-shop walls are lined with goofy souvenir taxidermy, like jackalopes, warthogs, and stuffed raccoons with their paws inside peanut butter jars. There's also something called a "Utah Werewolf"—a donkey's butt decorated with eyes and teeth. Don't ask.

You'll find the Fort Zion Virgin Trading Post at 1000 West Highway 9. Or call (435) 635-3455.

If Wile E. Coyote was ever thrown in jail, it might in be one like this.

SEVEN BRIDES
FOR ONE MAYOR

From Chicago's Richard J. Daley to Las Vegas' Oscar Goodman, the United States has seen a lot of colorful mayors. But few more so than Alex Joseph, the outspoken libertarian who founded the remote hamlet of Big Water and then built a polygamist enclave that attracted attention from around the world.

Joseph, who died of liver cancer in 1998 at age sixty-two, claimed to have wed twenty women, although by his death only seven wives remained. He famously said it was reading the Bible that persuaded him to try polygamy, not his brief stint as a member of the Mormon Church—although the LDS Church excommunicated him for it in 1969.

In the 1970s with a dozen wives in tow, the California native moved to the southern Utah desert near Lake Powell. His lifestyle raised eyebrows among local sheriffs, who kept a watchful eye on him for years. After a hard-fought campaign led by Joseph, the community was incorporated as Big Water in 1983. Joseph was named the town's first mayor and served in the job for eleven years, although he effectively ran the town after that, too. By the time of his death, he had twenty-one children and twenty-seven grandchildren.

A former Marine, cop, forest ranger, gold prospector, author, and boat captain, Joseph was a man of many interests and eccentricities. He once claimed to have done more than 2,000 baptisms for the dead from a houseboat in Lake Powell. He favored the decriminalization of marijuana, coined his own money, and carried a .357 Magnum with "For Christ's Sake" inscribed on the handle.

But it was polygamy for which he was best known. In contrast to most other Utah polygamists, who shun outsiders, Joseph welcomed the world to his eccentric fiefdom. Documentary film crews and TV shows such as Inside Edition visited the compound regularly, seeking titillating details about the family's sexual practices. Joseph always downplayed his unorthodox lifestyle.

"Polygamy comes naturally to a lot of men," he told anyone who would listen. "Jack Kennedy and I are the same. I just happened to have married all of mine."

INDEX

INDEX

INDEX

INDEX

INDEX

INDEX

INDEX

About the Author

Brandon Griggs has been writing for newspapers and magazines for more than two decades. In his twelve-plus years at *The Salt Lake Tribune* he has covered the NBA Finals, the Sundance Film Festival, the 2002 Winter Olympics, and the many ups and downs of Donny Osmond's career. He spent the 1999–2000 academic year as a fellow in the National Arts Journalism Program at Columbia University.

When he's not sweating a deadline, Brandon likes to explore Southern Utah's wilderness, listen to indie rock, follow the Boston Red Sox, and try in vain to keep up with the stacks of books on his nightstand. He lives in Salt Lake City with his wife, Kristy, and their cat, Mookie.